THE THOMPSON COUNTRY,

Being Notes on the History of Southern British Columbia, and Particularly of the City of Kamloops, Formerly Fort Thompson.

By

MARK S. WADE, M. D.

KAMLOOPS.

Inland Sentinel Print.

1907.

PREFACE.

Even amongst our own people, how little is known of the early history of British Columbia! That the Fur Traders were the first white men to take up permanent residence in the wilds of the unknown Interior land lying between the Rocky Mountains and the Pacific Ocean, is common knowledge, but, with that, error creeps in and with the very phrase "The Fur Traders" is associated the idea that by it is meant the Hudson's Bay Company, an idea at once prevalent and erroneous. Established by Royal Charter in 1670, the Hudson's Bay Company gradually extended their field of operations westward, but it was the North West Company, formed in 1787, that first pushed their way west of the Rockies. These rival companies swept the North, the South being harvested by a later concern known as the Mackina Company. Then came the founding of the American Fur Company by John Jacob Astor, of New York, in 1809, and his aborption of the Mackina Company two years later. With the whole South field in his control, Mr. Astor turned his eyes Westward, beyond the Rockies, to the Oregon or Columbia River, and formed the Pacific Fur Company, with headquarters at Astoria, afterwards Fort George when the Nor'-Westers secured possession, at the mouth of that great waterway. Thence traders branched out Northward even as the Nor'-Westers made their way South. That both these companies should reach what is now Kamloops about the same time, is, therefore, scarcely a matter for wonder, and when the vigorous Northerners devoured the Pacific Fur Co., the Farther West, rich in the coveted pelts, was theirs alone, and so remained, so far as the Interior was concerned, until the amalgamation of the Hudson's Bay and North-West Companies.

This little volume is the outcome of an article published in 1905 dealing, in the main, with the early history of Kamloops. To this has been added new matter and this narrative, with its many imperfections and shortcomings, is the result It is not presented as a complete history of that section of the country embraced in the title, but merely as a contribution throwing some light on the past. It may perchance serve others engaged in historical research as a beacon; to warn from what should be avoided and to guide whither there lies safety and knowledge.

The author acknowledges with thanks the courtesy of Rev. Father Morice for the use of several cuts from his excellent work the "History of the Northern Interior of British Columbia."

Kamloops, B. C., 1st March, 1907.

CONTENTS.

Sunday at Yale During Railway Construction—From a Drawing.

THE THOMPSON COUNTRY.

HE Southern Interior of British Columbia
is the home of several tribal subdivisions of
Indians of Salish stock, further subdivided
into bands, each band residing on some de-
finite location or reserve . Of these tribal
subdivisions the Shuswaps (Shoowha'pa-
mooh), possess the largest territory which
includes Shuswap and Adams Lakes, the valleys of the North and South Thompson rivers and the main Thompson nearly to Ashcroft, the Bonaparte river, Hat Creek, Clinton
and the valley of the Fraser from Pavilion
Creek to Soda Creek, their boundary being the territory
of that other great branch, the Tinneh or Dene tribe
Along the Fraser river valley below Pavilion live the
Lillooets (Sta'tlumooh), meeting the Thompsons near
Foster's bar on the Fraser, the Thompsons (Ntla-ka-pe-
mooh) being the western neighbors of the Shuswap·
and occupying the Similkameen district (excepting Kere-
meos which is Okanagan), the Nicola valley and that of
the Fraser from Foster's Bar to Spuzzum. The Okan-

agans (Ool-anakane) inhabit the country to the south
and east of the territory on the Shuswaps and Thompsons
The western leg of the Columbia valley, including Arrow
Lakes and Kootenay river, is claimed by the S-na-a-
chik'st, a subdivision of the Salish proper, their headquarters being, however, in Montana Their territory
divides the Okanagans from the Kootenays (Kootenuha)
The Salish proper were originally known as "Flat-heads"
When first discovered by Canadian voyageurs they had
amongst them slaves taken from the coast tribes where
the head was deformed

Little is known of the history of these aboriginal inhabitants prior to the advent of the fur traders, who were
the first whites to penetrate the Interior   The remote
past is shrouded in a cloud of tradition, superstition and
mythology   It is evident, however, judging from these
sources of information, that the different tribes were
constantly at war with one another, the stronger enslav-
ing the weaker as opportunity offered The northern races,
the Tinneh, were the more warlike and it was probably
a party of that race that, clad in the habiliments of
warriors on the warpath, long before the first white man
descended the Fraser or even beheld its waters, set out
from the Chilcoten country and made a sudden and un-
expected appearance in the Bonaparte valley. But the descent was made in the height of the salmon fishing season,
and, as provisions had been abnormally scarce during
the previous winter, all the Shuswaps, young and old, had
removed from their villages in the Bonaparte and Thompson valleys to their fishing grounds at Pavilion. Finding
none left in the villages where they had expected to surprise the stay-at-homes and enslave them, the stranger

Indian Salmon Cache.

warriors pursued their way south and finally reached a
point on the Thompson opposite the mouth of the Nicola
river   There they were discovered by scouts of the
Thompsons who at once carried the tidings of the presence
within their territory of a hostile force, to their fellow
tribesmen at Nicomen and Lytton.

A strong force of the Thompsons at once set out to
repel the invaders and having duly reconnoitred the enemy's position and estimated his strength, established
themselves in his front and rear   The invaders were not
slow to realise the danger that threatened them by a
superior force established in commanding positions and,
with admirable discretion, quietly and unobserved, crossed
the Thompson river under cover of night   They ascended
the Nicola, followed by the Thompsons who continually
harassed them, finally driving them into the Similkameen district   There, however, the strangers, young men
for the most part with their wives with them, took a
firm stand and offered such resolute resistance that their
pursuers ceased to interfere with them further   There
the newcomers remained and the Thompsons and Okanagans were subjected to conquest at their hands, not by
the warriors but by their women who were good to look
upon and found favor in the eyes of the young men
among the older established peoples.   Treaties were
made and inter-marriages resulted, and gradually the
strangers lost their individuality.   They are credited with
being the first inhabitants of the Similkameen of whom
there is any record

At what date the Indians of the Southern Interior
had their first knowledge of the whites there is no de-
finite information but it was probably at some time con-

Old Indian Graveyard.

siderably subsequent to the events narrated above Alexander Mackenzie, the first white man to descend the waters of the Upper Fraser, was informed by the Carrier Indians, a branch of the Tinnehs, that their immediate neighbors, the Shuswaps, were a malignant race, "who lived in subterranean recesses," and that they possessed iron arms and utensils which they had obtained from friendly tribes who had received them directly from the whites, probably from the coast Indians Mackenzie's historical journey took place in 1793, but it was not until afterwards that the Shuswaps had their first glimpse of the white man, the available evidence placing this event about the beginning of the last century. A Spokane chief, Pilakamulahuh, connected through his mother with both the Okanagans of Penticton, at the southern end of Okanagan lake, and the Shuswaps, had as one of his wives a Similkameen woman of Tinneh stock, in all probability a descendant of that adventurous band that had set out from the Chilcotin country as already related It was the custom in those days for the Indians living west of the Rocky Mountains and yet near enough to the prairies to engage in buffalo hunting, to band together for mutual protection against the common foe, the Blackfeet, when on those excursions, the Spokanes, Kootenuha, and sometimes the Nez Perces and Coeur D'Alenes, being among those so doing On one of these annual hunts they met a party of Canadian trappers at Hell Gate's Pass, near where Helena, Montana, now stands The two parties fraternized and when, towards the end of summer, the homeward journey westward across the Rocky Mountains was begun, two of the trappers, Finan Macdonald and Legace, accompanied them as guests of the Colville chief, who took them to his winter quarters at Kettle Forks on the Columbia river, where they ultimately married two of his daughters. Finan Macdonald, afterwards in 1812, had charge of a post among the Flatheads in the service of the Northwest Company

Late in the autumn, Pilakamulahuh went into winter quarters with his Similkameen wife at Penticton He entertained the other Indians of the village with tales of the whites met with on the buffalo hunt and his fame as a story-teller became so widespread that he was a welcome guest wherever he visited, his vivid descriptions of the white men and their doings proving particularly attractive In fact he found this occupation so agreeable that he did little else and made journeys far from his usual haunts to gratify his own vanity as a narrator and the curiosity of his eager listeners, a course that ultimately proved his undoing

The people of Shuswap invited him to visit them and tell them the wonderful things he had entertained his own people with First he went to Spallumcheen and it required a whole month to tell all he knew of the white people Next the inhabitants of the village of Kualt, Haltkam and Halaut, on Shuswap Lake and the South Thompson river, invited him in succession and at each place he spent a month. Tokane, the chief of the Kamloops band, also had him pay his village a visit and accorded him a grand reception.

This round of festivities and story telling occupied so much time that when spring came again Pilakamulahuh was not prepared to join the annual buffalo hunt on the plains. Instead, he accepted Tokane's invitation to spend the summer at the Shuswap's fishing grounds at Pavilion

on the Fraser this afforded him another and more excellent opportunity to tell his story of the wonderful
whites   There he met the chief of the Fountain band of
the Lillooets and by him was invited to visit his camp,
a few miles farther down the valley.   Nothing loth, the
now thoroughly seasoned narrator went and entertained
numerous visitors from below Lillooet and from villages
on the lakes west of that place, who had heard of the
marvels he related and came to hear them in person
One of them, the chief from Seton Lake, listened with
increasing incredulity to Pilakamulahuh describe these
beings with white skins, blue eyes, light, short, curly
hair; clad in woven material so fashioned as not to im-
pede their movements; armed with a weapon that killed
birds on the wing and at a great distance, shod so that
they could walk over cactus without being pricked.   All
these things the Seton Lake chief utterly disbelieved and
said so in plain language.   He further asserted that there
was no animal on which men could ride and outstrip the
buffalo; no weapon that discharged, with a noise as of
thunder and a smoke like fire, a missile so fast that the
eye could not see it.   In brief, he declared the honored
story-teller to be a liar and that the tales he related were
unworthy the attention of men and warriors.   Thus
grossly insulted, Pilakamulahuh reached for his bow and
arrows, intending to wipe out the affront with blood, but
his adversary was too quick for him and wounded him
with two arrows.   His friends the Shuswaps carried him
back to their own camp at Pavilion and there he died. Before the shadow of death fell upon him, however, he had
urged his son N'kuala, then a mere boy, to avenge his
murder.

By the time N'kuala reached manhood's estate, the whites had established a trading post at Spokane with outposts at other points tributary to it One of the latter was near the head of Okanagan Lake in charge of a Mr. Montigny, assisted by a man named Pion After a very successful winter's trading, Montigny departed for head-quarters with the furs, leaving everything at the post in the care of young N'kuala who had already earned a reputation and was a chief of some standing Upon his return, Montigny, finding everything safe and sound, rewarded N'kuala with a gift of ten guns, a supply of ammunition, tobacco and pipes Here was the young chief's opportunity During the winter he trained the best men of his tribe in the use of the guns From the traders who had established themselves at Walla-Walla he had received the gift of a horse. With firearms and a horse at his disposal, he felt prepared to undertake the task of avenging his father's death. Meeting the Shuswaps, Thompsons and Similkameens in solemn council, he invited them to join him in an attack on the Lillooets. They agreed without hesitation and, in the height of the salmon season, fell suddenly upon the unsuspecting Lillooets, killing over three hundred of then and taking many women and children prisoners Little resistance was offered the attack, the noise and deadly effect of the guns and the terrifying, to them, appearance of N'kuala on horseback riding from point to point directing the attack, completely demoralising the astonished Lillooets, In this striking manner was the truth of Pilak-amulahuh's narrative proved and his death avenged, To his allies, N'kuala gave a great feast at Nicola, driving a large herd of wapiti, which must then have been plen-

A Native Basket Maker.

tiful, into a corral where they were dispatched with spears, the antlers from the slaughtered animals forming two large heaps that endured until after the whites settled in the district

In many respects the Indians of to-day retain the customs of their ancestors but in others, notably their dwellings, clothing, and mode of burial, marked changes have taken place, the influence of the whites being apparent in these particulars The old village sites were carefully chosen, a sandy soil and a southern, sunny exposure being preferred. The dwellings among all the tribes inhabiting the drier portions of the Interior, were of the one type, called in the Chinook jargon, Keekwillee houses, which simply means underground houses. They were often of considerable size, were round in form and consisted essentially of a circular hole dug to a depth of about six feet and from twenty-five to thirty feet in diameter From the circumference a superstructure of timber was erected sloping towards the centre forming a cone shaped framework In this were interlaced boughs, bark, etc, the roof thus formed being further covered with soil. The entrance was at the peak of the roof, the same opening also serving as a chimney. A ladder, or notched pole facilitated ingress or egress These buildings formed the permanent quarters and were always occupied in winter months, a temporary dwelling made of poles covered with sheets of bark or animal skins serving the purpose of the primitive tribes at the hunting and fishing grounds These temporary residences are occasionally seen at this day but of the Keekwillee houses only the circular depression, showing the

site of some ancient village, now remain, the name
The Shuswaps, Okanagans, Thompsons and in fact
Keekwillee holes being given to the pits.
all the Interior tribes had then, as they still have, in common with the Tinnehs, Crees, and other Indians, sweat
houses. These consist of a number of willow boughs
planted in the ground at either end, half of them being
run at right angles to the others, all being fastened at
each point of intersection. Blankets, skins or other material covered the frame work thus made, all apertures
were carefully closed, and after placing inside a number
of heated stones and a vessel of water, the person about
to undergo the sweating process, crept within the dome
shaped structure, poured the water slowly on the hot
stones and endured the heated vapor that arose therefrom
until the sweating had proceeded long enough. The
sweat was generally ended with a plunge into river or
lake, the houses being built conveniently near water with
this end in view.

The Indian burial ground of the present day has no
resemblance to that of the old time native. They were
located near the permanent villages, sandhills being
chosen, no doubt, because the graves were more easily
dug in this loose soil. Unlike some of the coast tribes,
who disposed of their dead by placing them in boxes on
raised platforms or in trees, the Interior Indians interred
the dead in graves, many of the bodies being buried in
the sitting posture, others again being bent and then placed
on the side. Copper ornaments, dice made of beaver
teeth, pipes of stone rudely carved, portions of garments
made of sage brush bark and other fibrous material in
which the bodies were wrapped, red and yellow earths

for paint, arrow heads, etc, were usually found in the
many old graves that have been opened by archeologists,
who have ransacked every available burial ground and
removed the prehistoric implements, etc , found deposited
with the dead   A small shelter or tent-like house was
generally erected over a grave which- was usually enclosed.   Poles, painted and decorated with streamers,
sometimes carved, and carved and painted figures of men,
frequently adorned the old burial grounds and in later
days, after the whites had made such things possible,
pot and kettles and other articles were hung about the
grave.   The simple cross now ,takes the place of the
hetrogeneous collections of those past days.

,   Until the whites introduced, first, flint and steel and,
later, the lucifer match, the Interior Indians obtained
fire by friction, a wooden drill being turned between the
palms of the hands for this purpose, the point being
pressed against a piece of the dry root of the poplar
The sparks thus produced were caught upon tinder and
blown into a flame   Culinary operations were of
most primitive style.   -Possessing neither metal nor
earthenware pots, food , that required boiling wa.
placed in closely woven baskets which were filled with
water which was raised to the necessary heat by dropping
red hot stones into it.   Basket making was quite an art
with these people and a few of the older Indians still
do a little of it

Before the advent of the fur traders, furs and skins
of wild animals formed the clothing worn by the ma-
jority of the Indians, deerskin being a useful and favorite
material.   The fibre of the bark of the sage-brush was
used for making a cort of petticoat for the women Fea-

thers, shells, copper bracelets, strings of animals' teeth, etc., were used as ornaments for the person. The goods introduced by the Northwest Company and Hudson's Bay Company found favor in the eyes of the natives and speedily effected a radical dress reform in both sexes.

Bows and arrows and spears, were the weapons used in hunting, the arrow heads and spear points being made of stone, the same material being made into knives, chisels, and other implements. Needles were made of bone. Pipes were made from steatite and were generally ornamented with rude carvings and incised lines, similar decorations being found on other wooden, bone and soft stone tools and implements, the designs having meanings attached.

CHAPTER II.

THE COMING OF THE WHITE MEN.

The First Explorers into the Interior—Mackenzie's Jour-
ney—The Coming of Simon Fraser and David
Thompson—Founding of Fort Thompson
The Fur Traders—Rival Companies—
Exploration of the North Thomp-
son—The Philosophy of
Alexander Ross.

CHAPTER II.

THE COMING OF THE WHITE MEN.

HE early history of British Columbia is large-
coveries of a few intrepid, adventurous
ly an account of the explorations and dis-
spirits who made the unknown wastes and
wilds of the western slope of the continent
the field of their labors. By the sea the mar-
iners of Great Britain, Spain, Russia and the
United States had visited the North West
coast line of the Pacific, but what lay beyond that coast line, beyond those mountain
ranges that reared their heights in the back-
ground was unknown to them. This
knowledge was gained by the fur hunters, who were the
first explorers in the unknown west. The first of these
was Alexander Mackenzie, who made the first partial
descent of the Fraser as early as 1793, an expedition made
in the interests of the North West Company in whose
service he was. The hardships and well nigh insur-
mountable obstacles he encountered, and which would
have daunted a less bold spirit, are modestly told in his
journals.

The course followed by Mackenzie in his momentous and hazardous journey was up the Peace and Parsnip rivers; a short portage across the height of land separating the Mackenzie and Fraser watersheds; down "Bad river" a shallow, rocky and rapid stream which played havoc with the big canoe carrying the explorer and party, to the Great River, the Fraser This was descended as far as Alexandria, where Mackenzie was given a far from attractive description of the Shuswaps who were said to be "a very malignant race, who lived in large subterranean recesses " (Keekwillee houses).

The Shuswaps then possessed, so he was informed, iron utensils and arms procured from other Indians farther west, who in turn obtained them from whites at the coast

Reascending the Fraser to the mouth of the Blackwater, that stream was ascended, and finally the Pacific Ocean was reached at Bentinck Inlet, 22nd July, 1793 One month later, August 24th, the entire party was safely returned to Fort Chippewayan, the starting point

Following in his steps came another servant of the same great fur trading company, the Nor'Westers, Simon Fraser, and his explorations have exercised a material influence upon the history of the province. He did not confine himself to making explorations; he busied himself establishing trading posts and forts and gaining for his company a secure foothold in the fur trade in the virgin land. Thinking he had reached either the Columbia or one of its main tributaries, Fraser, in 1806, navigated the stream, established several forts and in the spring of 1808, in company with John Stuart and Jules Maurice Quesnel left Fort George, at the junction of the Fraser and Nechaco rivers, he set out to trace

Sir Alexander Mackenzie.

the river to its mouth It was not a pleasure trip as
they soon discovered In his journal, Fraser mentions
that having reached the village of the Askettihs, and
by this name he is presumed to mean the Lillooet
Indians, the men, who were dressed in coats of mail,
received him with a volley of arrows. The village he
describes as "a fortification one hundred feet by twenty-
four, surrounded by palisades eighteen feet high, slant-
ing inward, and lined with a shorter row, which sup-
ports a shade, covered with bark, constituting the dwellings "

They abandoned their canoes before they reached
the confluence with the Thompson river, where Lytton
is now situated, and the rest of the journey they did
on foot as far as the vicinity of what is now Yale,
where they secured a canoe and journeyed to the coast
in comfort and safety. Between Lytton and Yale he
was not long in finding evidences that the natives among
whom he was traveling, had, directly or indirectly
trafficked with other Europeans since articles of Eu-
ropean manufacture were seen at intervals. One of
these was "a copper kettle and a gun of a large size,
which are probably of Russian manufacture." Another
article was a huge sword made of sheet iron. After
arriving at their goal, the sea coast, it was considered
neither wise nor safe, on account of the troublesome
natives, to remain there long and after but one day's
rest, the return trip was commenced. Fort George had
been left on May 26th and they entered its portals on
August 6th, having in the meantime made the journey
to the coast and return over one of the most arduous
routes conceivable.

About the time that John Jacob Astor was fitting out his expedition on the Tonquin to establish the Pacific Fur Company at Astoria, at the mouth of the Columbia, David Thompson, a Welshman, like Alexander and Fraser a Nor' Wester, set out for the west, having already made several trips, penetrating 'the Rockies as early as 1800, and arrived at the Columbia river, in British Columbia, in January, 1811. Early in the spring he set out for the mouth of that great stream and reached Astoria on July, 15th, only to find that Mr Astor's expedition had arrived a few weeks before and were then engaged building their fort. He remained a few weeks for rest and then set out on the return journey and by way of Arrow Lakes and the Columbia, reached his starting point. It was during this expedition he descended the Thompson river and established Fort Thompson, afterwards named Fort Kamloops

British Columbia was then not know by that name; it was spoken of as New Caledonia, though by some, that portion of it north of Alexandria only was so called, the southern portion being named the Thompson district Farther south still was the Oregon country and it was from there that the next visitor came to Kamloops, or as it was then called, Fort Thompson, in 1812. This visitor was Alexander Ross, one of the members of the little community established at Astoria, at the mouth of the Columbia by the Pacific Fur Company of which Mr Astor was the leading spirit When in 1813 the North West Company acquired the property of the Astor company some of the men were given their choice of entering the service of the new

masters or accepting a free passage to New York or
Montreal Of those who chose to remain in the country
and the new service was Alexander Ross

With the change of owners Astoria changed also its
name and became known as Fort George, and from
that point, in the spring of 1814, the first great movement of the North West Company on the Columbia
was begun, the departure for the Interior, en route to
Fort William, of the spring brigade, consisting of four-
teen boats in which were embarked no fewer than 124
men, exclusive of the men of the Astor company who
had elected to return to Canada by land in preference
to making the voyage round the Horn, the whole leaving
the Fort with flags flying and the din of a general
salute ringing in their ears Ross and a little party
accompanied the brigade as far as Fort Okanagan where
they separated, the brigade continuing their journey
along the Columbia, Ross taking pack horses overland
back to his post at Kamloops In his first experience
at that point he must have encountered some competition from the North Westers for in his book, "The
Fur Hunters" he alludes to there "being now no rivalry
there." Of this second journey he says:—"From Okanagan I proceeded northward, some 300 miles, to my
own post at She-whaps There being now no rivalry
there, or elsewhere to contend with, I put the business
in train for the season, and immediately returned again,
with the view of being able to carry out a project of
discovery, which I and others had contemplated for
some time this was to penetrate across the land from
Okanagan, due west, to the Pacific, on foot, a distance
supposed not to exceed 200 miles; and for the perfor-

mance of which I had allowed two months"

The following season Ross again visited Kamloops and of that visit he says — "I set out for my post at the She-whaps, and reached that place in the month of August During my absence a man by the name of Charette, whom I had left in charge, had been murdered. The murderer was a young Indian lad who had been brought up at the establishment. They had gone on a trip to Fraser's river, six days' journey north, and had quarrelled one evening about making the encampment During the dispute the Indian had said nothing; but rising shortly afterwards, and laying hold of Charette's own gun, he suddenly turned round and shot him dead, without saying a word and then deliberately sat down again."

That winter, 1815-6, Ross spent fur hunting between She-whaps and Okanagan, returning to Fort George, as was the custom, in the spring for supplies, again going north to his old post in time for the winter trapping He recounts how on this journey one of his men, named Brusseau, fell sick and was unable to continue. The only course left was to make him comfortable, place him in charge of another man, leave a supply of food and let him remain until either recovery or death. As the case was considered hopeless, the nurse was given a spade with which to dig the grave should the sick man die. Ten days afterwards the nurse arrived at Kamloops with the news of his patient's death and as for the spade, the Indians had stolen it. All this passed for truth, until some time afterwards who should turn up but poor dead Brusseau, escorted by some friendly Indians. The nurse had become frightened at

the approach of Indians and had taken to his heels,
leaving the poor sick trapper to h s fate, and but for
the kindly offices of some natives he would have died.

The following year, 1817, Ross made a trip to Canoe
River in pursuance of orders from headquarters "to
examine the eastern section, lying between She-whaps
and the Rocky Mountains a large tract of wild country
never trodden before by the foot of any white man."
He took with him two of his trustiest men and two
Indians on foot and followed the North Thompson for
three days, then striling off through the timber north
of the valley The double journey took but 47 days
remarkably good time over a trail-less country, on foot,
packing on their backs the camp outfit and food. Of
the district he formed a very poor opinion.

Ross relates going a bear hunt with some of the local
chiefs shortly after his return from the journey to
Canoe river The fruit of the chase would be hailed
with delight by nimrods now-a-days. They only went
ten miles from the fort before they commenced operations and in two days the party killed seven bears,
nine wolves and eleven small deer "On these occa-
sions," says Ross, " they feel flattered by their trader
accompanying them. The party were all mounted on
horseback, to the number of seventy-three, and exhibited a fine display of horsemanship" One of the party,
"the chief Pacha of the hunting party," who rejoiced
in the name of Short Legs, was severely wounded in
the head by a female bear and Ross acted the part of
surgeon with some skill and considerable success, removing several portions of the skull from the wound, "I
extracted a bone measuring two inches long, of an oblong

form, and another of an inch square, with several
smaller pieces." In fifteen days the Indian, who was
after all a good for nothing, was up and about, to the
delight of himself and his near relations, but to the
disgust of the men at the fort against whom he was
constantly plotting.

This trader who for so many years did honors at
Kamloops gives the details of many adventures and
throws much light upon what were considered the
duties, troubles and pleasures of the fur trader's life.
"And one of the greatest pleasures, here alluded to,
consists in doing homage to the great. A chief arrives;
the honor of waiting upon him in a servile capacity falls
to your share, if you are not above your business.
You go forth to meet him; you invite him in; see him
seated; and if need require it, you untie his shoes, and
dry his socks. You next hand him food, water and
tobacco; and you must smoke along with him. After
which, you must listen with grave attention to all he
has got to say on Indian topics, and show your sense
of the value of his information by giving him some
trinkets, and sometimes even articles of value, in return.
But the grand point of all this ceremony is to know
how far you should go in these matters, and when you
should stop. By overdoing the thing, you may entail
on yourself endless troubles. When not employed in
exploring new and unfrequented parts, involved in diffi-
culties with the natives, or finding opposition in trade,
the general routine of dealing with most Indians goes
on smoothly. Each trading post has its leader, its in-
terpreter, and its own complement of hands; and when
things are put in proper train, according to the customs

Simon Fraser.

of the country, the business of the year proceeds without much trouble, and leaves you sufficient time for recreation You take your gun on your back; you can instruct your family, or improve yourself in reading and reflection, you can enjoy the pleasures of religion to better advantage, serve your God to more perfection, and be a far better Christian than were your lot cast in the midst of the temptations of a busy world."

The first pioneers received their supplies overland from Montreal via Fort William and across the continent by canoe and portage; a long wearisome journey and they so continued to get their supplies until the desirability of a more expeditious mode became sufficiently recognized The Pacific Fur Company had shown the feasibility of taking supplies from the coast into the interior of the Thompson district. She-whaps as Ross called it, by way of the Columbia to Fort Okanagan and thence by pack animals overland to their fort at Kamloops In 1821 this route was adopted for carrying supplies to the forts in New Caledonia, a distributing station being established at Alexandria on the Fraser. To that point the pack trains went from Kamloops, following the Kamloops ·Lake to Copper Creek, opposite Savona, ascending that stream across the hills to Deadman's Creek, and then by way of Loon Lake and Green Lake on to Alexandria To Alexandria came the boats and canoes from the post at Fort George, Fort James, etc, and received supplies brought by the pack trains, by which, in turn, the pelts gathered at the northern forts were taken south and ultimately reached Fort Vancouver, which in 1824 had superseded the post at Astoria From Fort Vancouver the furs were taken round the Horn by the vessels that brought the enormous supplies required for the system of posts in Oregon, Thompson and New Caledonia

Kamloops was the capital of the Thompson district and the fort was strongly palisaded, within the stockade there was room for the large horse brigades employed in the transportation of furs and goods. These pack trains were large affairs, numbering from 200 to 300 animals. In the winter season they were turned out on the hills near the fort where there was then abundant pasture and in the spring the band was gathered in, fat and sleek

John Tod successively officer in charge of the Hudson's Bay posts of Fort Alexandria and Kamloops, has graphically described the operating of the "brigades," incidently throwing a sidelight upon the Indian character. He says

"It was found convenient to take the annual produce of the trade of New Caledonia and the districts immediately south of it, on pack horses, southerly to the shipping place at Fort Vancouver on the Columbia river. This was the cheapest, indeed the only method. The country, for the most part, was easily traversed and furnished grass for pasture. The long journeying of this noble cavalcade of 400 or 500 horses, with their numerous attendants, drafted from various stations, took place annually at a stated time, 200 horses were kept at Fort Alexandria for the transport and I was always ready to join forces with my large contingent when the cavalcade reached Kamloops. Each officer, however,, retained control of his own horses. A "brigade" as applied in this organization consisted of 16 horses in charge of two men

The horses so banded kept together and each had its name
The load for each horse was two "pieces" of 84 pounds
each, and the horse was supposed to convey this about
20 miles a day, but, in fact, the distances between camping places varied

"I remember on one of the above periodical journeys
'a little incident which shows the importance of conciliating
and trusting the Indians. It was customary for a number
of these people to meet this regular cavalcade at the forks
of Okanagan river, not so much for trade as to exchange
civilities. Jogging along towards that place three Indians,
dressed in their best, accosted me with an invitation to
camp near their party, but added that they thought it
right to inform me that several notorious Indian horse
thieves had come among them, over whom they had not
the same power as over their own people. My reply
being that I would camp in their midst, they went off well
pleased On my telling this arrangement to my co-officer
of the cavalcade he became angry, drew out his horses
from it, and went to seek an encampment that would not
be, as he said, "among a lot of horse thieves" About
1,000 Indians were present at the Forks, and the evening
scene was picturesque. To my fire a number of chiefs
came, and there were many stories and abundant mirth-
fulness, finally, before retiring, and after a distribution of
tobacco, I made a speech in a manner they like, and wound
up by stating that my men had for two nights lost their
rest, and we were now going to have a good sleep, leaving horses and everything in the Indians' care They
sent the horses to some good pasture, and next morning
though I had some misgivings during the night, every
horse was brought to the camp.

Dispatching the loaded train, and having the usual half hour's chat with the chiefs before starting, I cantered along to my co-officer, who seemed in an excited state— the stem of his big pipe in his hand and the bowl swinging by the string, as he strode bridle over arm, gesticulating and swearing. "Hello!" said I, "what's up?" "Those cursed horse thieves," was the gruff reply, "have taken three of my horses, and they took two of them last night before they were unladen. How many have you lost?" "Not a one," said I.

CHAPTER III.

SUPERSTITION AND TRAGEDY.

A Hudson's Bay Grandee—Murder of Samuel Black at
Fort Kamloops—John Tod's Narrative.

CHAPTER III.

SUPERSTITION AND TRAGEDY.

FTER making his trip to Canoe River from Kamloops in 1817, Ross returned to Astoria and did not again visit his old post at She-whaps. From 1817 there is no available record of his successor, the next trader mentioned in charge of the post being John McLeod, who ruled it from 1822 to 1826, and when Sir George Simpson visited Fort Thompson October 6th, 1828, he found trader Ermatinger in charge. As resident governor of the Hudson's Bay Company Sir George Simpson made frequent journeys to all parts of the vast domain ocupied by that corporation. His visit to Fort Thompson, or Kamloops, was on one of these journeys, the most lengthy he had undertaken, extending from York Factory on Hudson's Bay to Fort Langley on the Fraser river. The entire distance was covered in ninety days, a remarkably short period, taking the transportation facilities obtainable into consideration —canoes, sometimes traveling on foot, and occasionally on horseback as, for example, on the trip from Alexandria to Kamloops. At Kamloops water transportation was re-

sumed, the journey from that point to the junction of the
Thompson and Fraser rivers, where Lytton now is, being
made in a canoe with twelve men paddling, an undertaking
fraught with danger in many places and requiring
great skill in handling the craft in turbulent waters to ac-
complish safely.

The next recorded ruler of the Kamloops district
was Samuel Black. Black was a Scotchman and once entertained a distinguished fellow countryman, David Douglas, the noted botanist, at the fort. It is related that
over the nightly cup of toddy, probably replenish-
ed several times, the guest bluntly told his
host that in his opinion the fur traders had
not a soul above a beaver skin, whereupon Black took
instant fire and challenged Douglas to mortal combat,
but the latter took his departure early in the morning
and so avoided the duel. In 1841 Tho'npson district
was added to New Caledonia. During the winter of
1841-2, Black was foully murdered by a nephew of a
deceased friendly chief, named Wanquille, on the excuse
that the trader had charmed Wanquille's life away

The circumstances attending the tragic death of
Black are given in detail by John Tod as follows:

"I was appointed as officer in charge of Fort Alexandria, on Fraser river, five or six hundred miles (longer by trail) northwest, in the direction of my old habitat
of New Caledonia. The "fort" was a stockade enclos-
ure with a block house and the usual buildings. It was
close to the bank amid dark forests. The road thither,
after about 300 miles, led past the important Hudson's
Bay Co.'s station at the junction of the north and south
branches of Thompson river, so named by Mr. David

Sir George Simpson.

Thompson, a Hudson's Bay man, who, while in the service of the Northwest Company, spent most of the time between 1808 and 1812 as a trader and explorer west of the Rocky Mountains, discovering in 1811 the northern head waters of the Columbia, which river he followed to the ocean The Indians called the place 'Kahm-o-loops,' meaning 'the meeting of the waters,' and we, less poetically, called it the 'Forks' of the Thompson

"The fort was on the right bank of the North Thompson at its mouth, opposite the modern village, or town, of Kamloops

"The surrounding country, in its general character, presents south of the river a rolling, open surface, the valleys clear, save for aspen poplars along the streams, and the uplands sparsely timbered, chiefly with 'red or 'bull' pines. It is more a pastoral than an agr cultural district, irrigation being necessary in most parts for cultivation. The officer in charge of the fort, Mr Black, a chief trader, gave me a hearty welcome during the day of my stay there Some calamitous presage, which I never could acount for, affected me on bidd ng him, good bye next morning, but passed away as we proceeded on our journey

"A few weeks later, being at Alexandria on a dark night in February, a French-Canadian showing the traces of a hard journey, entered the fort and said: 'Mr Black is murdered and all the men at Kamloops fort have fled in different directions '

"I may anticipate a little by stating here the facts of this tragic occurrence, as these have been wrongly described in the book of his journey round the world in 1841-2, by the Governor, Sir George Simpson, who was at Fort Vancouver, on the Columbia river, in the middle of 1841, several months after it happened, and also described wrongly by other writers.

"A chief named Tranquille, of an Indian tribe near the fort, had died lately, and the widow, in her grief and concern for the departed, had told her son, a fine youth of 18, well disposed and quiet, that the father's spirit should be accompanied by the spirit of some chief of equal rank. This was urged daily until the youth, worn by importunity and a supposed sense of duty to his deceased father, seized his gun and sat himself down moodily in the hall of the Kamloops fort. Something in his appearance caused a servant to remark to Mr. Black that the Indian looked dangerous, but the latter said that probably the boy was ailing. Soon afterward, on Mr. Black crossing the hall from one room toward another, the Indian suddenly rose and fired at his back, and the bullet passed through the victim's heart and body and lodged in the wall.

"But to return. On hearing the French-Canadian's report, I directed him and two other men to start with me at dawn on horseback, with relays, from Alexandria for Kamloops. There were two feet of snow on the ground during the first part of our trip of 270 miles, and after a long week of almost incessant travel, or 'march,' as the word was, we reached our destination, to find Fort Kamloops abandoned save for the widow and children still weeping over Mr. Black's frozen body, lying where it fell. An Indian named Lolo, but, as a 'mission' Indian, who preached about St. Paul, commonly called 'Paul,' who had been occasionally employed at the fort, appeared soon to sympathize with us, and, possibly, to report proceedings to the Indians, whose neighboring camp was silent

"After examining as far as might be the course of the bullet, we buried the body, ascertained the murderer's name from Lolo, and then began to make an inventory of the goods at the fort. These seemed to be intact

"Several days were thus occupied, during which an armed Hudson's Bay Company party arrived from Fort Colville, and later another armed party from Fort Vancouver (to which southern place some of the men fleeing from the fort had gone), the expectation being that the Indians would be found in possession of the Kamloops fort. As my own station at Alexandria demanded my care, I returned thither at once in these circumstances, but the end was not yet.

"The party from headquarters at Fort Vancouver began to terrorize the Indians within reach of Kamloops as a means of enforcing delivery of the murderer Horses were seized, property destroyed, and, practically, short of killing men, war against the people was undertaken The result of this ill-judged action, of course, was nil, except in causing bitterness, and, after a time, the company's forces were recalled to Fort Vancouver and Colville A council held at the former fort, at which, as I said, the governor-in-chief was present, then decided on the policy to be adopted

"Obviously with hostile Indians intervening, the year's pack of furs from the interior of New Caledonia, which required a cavalcade of 400 laden horses, could not reach the shipping depot at Fort Vancouver, nor could the posts receive thence their goods for next year's trade Accordingly a temporising policy was approved.

"I was transferred from Alexandria to succeed Mr Black at Kamloops, with instructions to try to continue trading and the business of the district as usual, and with the intimation that toward the end of the year a well armed force would be sent to aid me in 'prosecuting hostilities.'

"As the above policy of the authorities seemed to me unnecessary and also dangerously provocative, in view of the number and boldness of the Indians, though not all of them had guns or much ammunition, or the wherewithal to purchase warlike equipment, I asked for, and was given rather grudgingly, more or less a free hand in the circumstances, and I shall now relate what took place, not for self-praise, but to illustrate how not to make an Indian war.

"Despatching Lolo, the Indian already mentioned (he was a man of birth and undoubted courage, but I never fully trusted him), to the different camps and tribes, I ascertained what horses had been taken from each and what property had been destroyed by the punitive expeditions, and I returned the horses from the bands at the fort and paid for the property in every case that was substantiated. Then I offered a bale of 'goods' to anyone who would show me or my agents where the murderer was; I desired no other help.

"On the third night after this notification an Indian called me up to say that his friends had decided to permit him to act as a guide, but he was to take no pay, in goods or otherwise. The murderer was far away in a valley covered with prickly pears, encamped there near a stream and guarded by twelve warriors. His information proved to be correct, for on my sending, with a guide, a small

party of three men (advisedly small in pursuance of my
own policy of regarding the matter as individual and not
tribal) the place was reached, but though the guards and
the murderer's wife and two child girls were there, he
himself, unwitting of the present pursuit, had visited the
Fraser river to buy salmon.   Indiscreetly, as I considered, the party seized one of the children and brought
her back to the Kamloops fort, whither they returned for
supplies and further orders.   I caused the child to be
dressed prettily from goods in the store, supplied with
a bag of toys, and immediately conveyed back to her mother by a special messenger on horseback.

"The latter remained a day at the camp, to which
the murderer had not returned), and before departing
homeward was told by the 'guards' that they would pro-
tect the man no longer, but would go home.   Thus the
youth became an outcast among his own people, with
his doom fixed and the avenger on his track, but it was
not until four or five months after this that he was run
down and killed, as I shall now relate.

"The pursuers, guided by the informant, came to the
crest of a hill and looked down on a small encampment
on the opposite side of a river in the valley.   The guide
said: "There is his place and the ford is in front of the
camp." Acordingly, when night fell, creeping to the river
side, they crossed, the guide a little ahead, when he
stopped to whisper, 'Hush! they are talking in the lodge
—two men's voices—one man, the man we want, is telling
of his dream that the white men were hanging him.'

"In the rush one inmate of the lodge was seized by
the throat; the other inmate dashed through the doorway,
escaping the clutch of the foreman of the pursuers on his

hair, as it had been cut short, but the foreman, a swift Scotchman, overtook and knocked him down with the butt of a gun. This fugitive was the murderer.

"Quickly he was taken across the ford in the river, tied securely on a horse, and the party traveled homeward on their four days' march, and finally reached a ferry on the Thompson river, which would save a round of several miles. A pipe was there smoked, and the foreman pondered over the risk of putting the prisoner in a canoe—finally he sent an armed man to the other side, and placed in the canoe one paddler in the stern, another in the bow, and the prisoner in the middle, not tying the hands of the latter. About the middle of the stream the prisoner upset the canoe, and, after diving, swam to the opposite side. The guard there, with levelled gun, ordered him to go back. 'Let me land,' pleaded the murderer 'If they had killed me at the time of the deed it would have been well; now I wish to live,' whereupon the guard fired, wounding him in the hand. He wailed and turned into the water, and the current took him down stream within short gun range of the foreman and another man at a point, or spit, of gravel, from which they shot and killed him, he crying out before he sank that he did not wish his death avenged."

It is stated by a grandson of the murdered trader that Black was buried at the fort, the body being wrapped in a horse hide and enclosed in a box made of hewn boards. When the next brigade set out for the trip south, it was decided to send Black's body with it to the Dalles. Early in the journey it became necessary to convey the furs, and Black's body, across a stream on foot, a tree felled across it serving as a bridge. While making the passage over this narrow footway with the heavy and cumbersome box containing the body, one of the Indians bearing it slipped and Indians and box fell into the stream Before it was extracted, the water had penetrated every portion of the interior and had such an effect as to render it impossible to carry out the original determination to convey the remains to headquarters and the unfortunate body was again buried, this time at Ducks, where it has since rested undisturbed.

CHAPTER IV.

THE REIGN OF JOHN TOD.

Building a Second Fort—Tod's Resourcefulness—Vaccina-
tion in a New Role—A Hostile Chief.

CHAPTER IV.

THE REIGN OF JOHN TOD.

OLLOWING Samuel Black came John Tod. He is described as being a man possessing neither good looks, nor learned, polished nor refined, and as having lapsed into a stage of semi-savagery. In physique he was tall, wiry, with facial characteristics of the race of which he was a son, the Scottish. But in spite of personal drawbacks and deficiencies he was a man from the ground up, with a powerful arm and a strong will to help it out. The original fort was built on the flat at the north side of the Thompson river in the angle formed by that stream and the North river. Tod built a new one on the opposite side of the main stream, differing little from the forts afterwards built at other points by the Hudson's Bay Company. It consisted of seven buildings, used as stores, dwellings and shops, enclosed within palisades 15 feet high, with gates on two sides and bastions at two opposite angles. To the older building were added strongly stockaded corrals for the hundreds of horses bred and kept at this post. Within the

fort dwelt the chief trader with his Indian wife and
their three children, half a dozen men and a halfbreed
boy. Protected only by this small force, a large stock
of trinkets and supplies of all kinds were kept on hand
with which to trade with the Indians, to the number of
several hundreds, who made Kamloops their trading
point. Seven tribes traded here, coming from Kootenay,
Okanagan, Similkameen, and other distant illahies for
that purpose.

Towering 2,000 feet above the valley of the Thompson
and overlooking Kamloops city is a large eminence
known as Mount St. Paul. It bears its name from a
certain Shuswap chief, given that same name by the
traders and the company's men but christened Jean
Baptiste Lolo by the missionary Catholic priests, for
already they had visited the post, Father Demers, who
afterwards became bishop, visiting it in 1845, the year
before John Tod began his reign. Lolo lived near the
fort and enjoyed almost absolute authority over his
people. The regular winter supply of salmon for use
at the fort and by the Indians was procured, not from
the waters of the Thompson, but from the Indians at
the Fountain, on the Fraser river, a few miles above
Lillooet. It was arranged that Lolo should e d a
party of men and Indians, for the annual fish
supply and in due time a start was made. Greatly to
Tod's surprise two days later Lolo returned, alone, and
after a good deal of beating about the bush, for the
red man is not a lover of direct methods when more
circuitous way can be used, it transpired that he had
learned of a conspiracy entered into by over 300 Indians,
all members of the Shuswap tribe, to capture the fort

John Tod.

at Kamloops and after murdering the inmates, rob it
of its contents. Tod knew nothing of fear, was resource-
ful and had a thorough knowledge of the native character and his mind was soon made up. He briefly ex-
plained the situation to his wife, wrote a full explanation
addressed to his superior officers in case he should fall,
and bidding the halfbreed saddle two of his swiftest
horses, while Lolo was asleep in his own lodge, with
that one lad as his sole attendant, he set out to quell
the threatened rising.

Lolo had a covetous eye upon a certain sorrel horse
belonging to Tod and as he had made a request for
this animal when reporting the conspiracy, a request
brusquely refused, it was a matter for conjecture
whether the alleged uprising was a mere piece of decep-
tion to gain the horse as a reward for a fancied service,
or whether he had the stern reality before him By
hard riding he overtook the party from Kamloops, at
the point Lolo had left them, by noon and found they
had no knowledge of the conspiracy, though he discovered this without letting them become aware of it
Orders were given to look well to the condition of their
arms and next morning they moved forward, and pres-
ently, on reaching an open space, he detected signs of
opposition; painted armed savages lurking behind trees
and bushes; men only, lack of women and children
clearly indicating a war party. Calling to him a Canadian named George Simpson, he bade him fall back
quietly with the horses and should disaster befall, to
ride to the fort as quickly as possible. Simpson hesi-
tated and wanted to share the danger "Damn you,
go," roared Tod Then he carried out his scheme, daring

as it was simple. Riding at full speed towards the war party, who raised their weapons to pour a volley that would have torn him to pieces had it been fired, he drew his sword and pistols, raised them aloft and then deliberately threw them on the ground. Then, unarmed, alone, he made his horse perform all manner of evolutions, and while the Indians gazed, curious as to what would happen next, he charged into their midst. He smiled at them but they knew him and saw his smile was of anger, not mirth. He demanded what they wanted. "We want to see Lolo. Where is he?" they demanded in turn. "Then you have not heard the news? Poor Lolo, he is at home sick," he replied and then proceeded to tell them that Lolo had the smallpox! They had heard of the dread scourge and they had learned, too, of the way it had decimated the Indians of Oregon after the Whitman massacre; a punishment sent by the gods for wrong doing! He told them how much he loved his red brothers, that they must not come near the fort until he gave them notice and that he had brought medicine to keep them from dying from the disease they dreaded so much. There was a complete revulsion of feeling; the man they would have cheerfully killed, they hailed as their savior and flew to obey him when he bade them load his horses with salmon. He kept them employed while this was being done and then vaccinated as many as his supply of virus would suffice, instructing them how to vaccinate others from the vesicles when they became ripe. And so ended the great Shuswap conspiracy and, needless to say, Lolo received the sorrel he had so long and ardently coveted.

In the "History of British Columbia" Bancroft relates with precise detail an entertaining story of how
Tod subdued some unruly Indians by threatening to blow
them all to pieces—and the country besides—by explod-
ing three kegs of gunpowder   The facts as related by
Tod himself are somewhat at variance with the historian's
picturesque tale, but although the actual occurrence was
less romantic than Bancroft's version of it, it is interest-
ing enough and serves to show the need of constant
alertness on the part of these isolated fur traders in order
to carry them through with safety and without loss of
dignity and influence

The changes, and rumors of changes, in the company's business in the western department consequent
upon the Oregan Treaty of 1846, tended to disturb the
Indian mind as to the future, though these changes, practically, did not affect a band of Indians trading usually
at the fort, but which did not affiliate with the Indians of
any "nation" permitted by Tod to encamp in the neigh-
borhood while waiting to proceed to a distant hunting
ground on a further opening of the spring season

The news spread widely, even so far as Okanagan
Forks over 200 miles distant south   "Nicola," a very
great chieftain and a bold man, for he had 17 wives,"
naively writes the trader, "ruled the Indians there, and
claimed lordship over a territory as big as the half of
Scotland, stretching far into the present British Columbia, an administrative dstrict which still bears his name.
The band permitted to encamp was, unfortunately, the
hereditary enemy of Nicola's people.   The old chief sat
for two days pondering, then jumped up and spoke to his
warriors of the misdeeds of the encamping tribe which

had ventured into land under his own (claimed) jurisdiction, and he urged them, if they had the hearts of men and not of women, to wipe out those people. "Let us march!" exclaimed the young men. "Nay, not yet!" interposed Nicola, "for we lack ammunition."

What happened is thus related by Tod:

"My first hint of impending mischief was the desire of an Indian for a gun and a quantity of ammunition as the price of ten skins, instead of, as usual, taking blankets and cloth as pay of the barter. 'We are going to the Blackfeet country,' said he. Next week another came with the same story, but by that time I had heard of Nicola's speech and said I had no ammunition to spare, whereupon, leaving his bundle of furs in the store, the Indian hurried back to Nicola to report progress, or rather failure, which so confounded the old chief that he again sat, for several days, I was told, in meditation. 'This man of the Kamloops fort,' finally said he, in a great speech, 'shelters our enemies and refuses to trade; we will take the fort and all there is in it and have our revenge on our enemies.' Spies told me of this decision and of the approach of the Nicola war party, painted and prancing along the bank of the South Thompson river, which caused the half-dozen French Canadians at the fort to flee hurriedly—though the wife of one upbraided him as a coward—and caused many other white men who were near to depart, as also the encamped band that was the cause of the mischief.

"It was now my turn, like the old chief, Nicola, to sit down and ponder, but my pondering occupied minutes instead of days. Seizing an Indian who passed the fort gate on foot, I dragged him roughly inside and compelled him to bring from the store a barrel of gunpowder and place it near the door   Then opening the barrel, I spilled the contents all over the doorway and directed the Indian to bring me a flint and steel, on which request he bolted, but I caught him, saying 'Not yet; I only wish to see that the flint will act'   We tried several and at last got a good apparatus   Thrusting the man out of the fort, I then laid a train of powder to the mass of it and sat down to wait   In about an hour the local Indian, Lolo, or Paul, with a Nicola Indian from the war party—the latter whitewashed as when not meditating a war parley—approached in a canoe   These I addressed from the bank of the river at the fort, driving them off with reproaches   'Begone, and quick! I want not you, where is that woman chief of yours?   Where is he   I am alone here, and Nicola fears with his whole tribe to attack a single man,' and so forth   That was the 'barrel of powder' incident.

"Nicola, to whom the Indian who had seen the powder spilling ran, held councils but did not risk an attack. The Indians knew the effect of a flask exploded, but a barrel, they conceived, might devastate the whole district   The end of the matter followed the practice in such cases of the civilized nations   Several of Nicola's principal chiefs who knew me came in peaceful array with assurances that he had only been conducting a "reconnaissance in force," and was pleased to know that the enemies of his people had departed; his respect for the great company and its honorable local manager was immense, it was a misapprehension that he ever contemplated an entry into the fort without invitation; but he, personally, hoped for an opportunity of enjoying that satisfaction

66

according to recognized etiquette before departing for the south. So I swept up the powder and entertained as best I could the baffled chieftain. He was a stately personage, the very pink of courtesy, who sat his horse like a crusader and commanded the entire devotion of his followers in any enterprise that did not involve the experimental personal test of an unknown explosive power."

CHAPTER V.

A NEW OUTLET.

Tod's Diplomacy with the Indians—The Oregon Treaty—
End of Dual Occupancy of Oregon.

CHAPTER V.

A NEW OUTLET.

HE unrest naturally felt by the Hudson's Bay Co., on account of the doubtful result of the diplomatic discussions respecting the international boundary caused the transfer of a number of horses, and also cattle from districts south of the 49th parallel to the Kamloops station, where bunch grass pasture was plentiful. Some of these came from Tod's old farming station on the Cowlitz, and he amused himself with the pretence that they recognized him. **Two hundred brood mares were** included in the great band thus sent to Kamloops, and in the spring, foals began to appear.

Unfortunately, also, there soon appeared an addition to the bands of wolves in the locality, as if these beasts of prey had been following the progress of the diplomatic negotiations. Vigilance was useless, but having heard of strychnine, Mr Tod sent to Walla Walla, 300 miles away, for a supply of it. The sequel is best told by the trader himself

"It happened that about this time I had three parties out in different places squaring logs to make new buildings, and to these I gave horse flesh and portions of the poison for wolf baits, enjoining them strictly to take the baits up every morning A man, Lamille, from one of these wood camps, on his way to the fort for a supply of provisions, placed, foolishly, a remnant of salt salmon he had with him on one of these wolf baits as he passed it, which bait had not been removed Later on a hungry Indian, seeing the morsel, kindled a fire and ate, not only the salmon, but the horse flesh wolf bait (which perhaps I should have marked), and when Camille, on returning that way, noticed the head of the Indian rising and falling in the long grass, he bethought him of the poison, and galloped back to the fort to tell me what he had seen

Seldom had I been in such a difficulty as then What to do I knew not, but, running to the medicine chest, I took out some blue vitrol and we hastened to the scene The Indian's teeth were set, but by forcing his jaws open a little I poured the vitrol down his throat This almost immediately caused violent vomiting and he survived, but was an invalid for a considerable time

The Indians generally, meanwhile, had been talking about the poison and this mishap to one of their number added much to their uneasiness Several hundreds in a state of excitement and alarm, but not in war dress, appeared at the fort to demand explanations Speech after speech was made by the chiefs—the fear evidently being entertained that I meditated poisoning the people. "What," said I in reply, "what do you suppose I am living among you for? Is it not to obtain furs and to trade? How could I get the furs if you were poisoned? Had I desired to poison you I could have done it long

A. C. Anderson.

ago. You know that I sent for the poison to kill the wolves that were killing the foals—your foals as well as mine" Then, perceiving the entry into the hall of the man who had taken the poison, I seized him, and, dragging him forward, said· "Here is the cause of your trouble—this thief who steals the white man's provisions—such a hungry thief that he will eat what is meant to kill wolves."

This diversion and attack saved the situation, for the poor wretch technically had committed two offences condemned by tribal sentiment—he had robbed from a white man and he had robbed what was akin to a "trap," and, moreover, he had stirred others against me, who had saved his own life lately by the exercise of wonderful medical skill, though I had burned his gullet in the process I was not pleased with my own argument, but it served the purpose"

While Tod, however, had charge of the fort, on May 15th, 1846, A C. Anderson, who then had charge of Fort Alexandria, the most southerly post on the Fraser except Fort Langley, set out with five men detailed for the purpose, to survey a new route of travel to the coast He had realised that the negotiations then pending between the governments of Great Britain and the United States with respect to the international boundary, would result in a new distributing point being selected on British soil to take the place of Fort Vancouver, which had for some time proved unsatisfactory on account of the anomalous position in which the company found themselves by reason of the dual occupancy of the territory in dispute. Should such a new post be created, a way of reaching it from Alexandria would be a neces-

city They passed down Kamloops lake, where they
made their first camp; crossed Deadman's creek in
an old canoe and made their way to the Bonaparte,
camping at Hat creek Next day they traversed the
Marble canyon, reaching Pavilion rancherie and following the Fraser to the Fountain. Arrived at Lillooet they
crossed the Fraser, followed Seton lake, Anderson lake,
and Lillooet and Harrison lakes to the Fraser again,
arriving at Fort Langley on May 24th He had been
unable to bring horses farther than Fountain and had
sent them to the Similkameen country, there to await
him.

On May 28th he again left Fort Langley and attempted
to find a way over the Hope mountains to the Nicola
country After trying several passes he fell in with a
Thompson river Indian who agreed to act as guide,
but he was not of much service. Finally the party
arrived at Vermilion Bay where they found their horses
awaiting them, and easily made their way to Kamloops
via Nicola lake, arriving at the fort on 9th June. Anderson was not satisfied, however, and next year he sought
to find a better way Leaving Kamloops with five men
he went to Nicola lake and followed the Nicola river
to its junction with the Thompson Thence he followed
the Thompson to the Indian village that stood where
Lytton now is, and made his way down the Fraser as
far as the village of the Sachincos (Yale). A trip by
canoe to Langley did not delay them long, and then
began the return journey. At Kequeloose, a point a
short distance above Spuzzum, a short cut was taken
across the mountains to Nicola lake and thence back
to Kamloops

Early in 1848 Fort Yale was established by Chief
Factor James Murray Yale then in charge of Fort Langley, and who had entered the service of the company
in 1815 Short in stature he was know as Little Yale
to the officers of the company, but in everything save
physique he was a giant; brave, fearless, reckless, he
was possessed of good administrative ability. It was
the conclusion of the Oregon treaty which placed the
international boundary line far north of Fort Vancouver,
and the unrest that followed the hostilities consequent
to the Whitman massacre that caused orders to be
issued to all Interior posts to proceed to Fort Langley
in 1848 for their supplies instead of to Fort Vancouver
Three brigades set out, one from Alexandria, one from
Kan loops and one from Colville; the route they were
to follow was that traversed the preceding summer by
Anderson But it proved a disastrous road and it was
condemned, the route by Hope being chosen instead,
and Fort Hope was built during the winter of 1848-9
The road was made the next season and, under the
name of the Hope Trail, was followed until 1860 when
the government road was made To those who see Hope
now it will come as a suprise to learn that in that year,
1860, it was the second largest town on the mainland,
it was for. a time a rendezvous for the gold miners
going to and returning from the Upper Fraser mines
and Cariboo, one authority asserting "and a number
of Chinese have taken up their abode in it It is making
rapid progress, and roads are being pushed forward
north and east of it."

Chief Trader, Paul Fraser, a son of Simon Fraser,
the discoverer and explorer, was placed in charge of

Fort Kamloops in the early 50's He was born at Glengarry, Ontario, and entered the service of the Hudson's Bay Company when nineteen years of age He was not a popular officer, being too curt and overbearing, not alone towards his subordinates, but to his brother officers as well The Hudson's Bay people had a method of their own of enforcing discipline and punishing misdemeanors by the indiscriminate flogging and beating of the Indians and halfbreeds. Paul Fraser had ample faith in the efficiency of this summary administration of "club" law, and was considered a capable officer, for this reason, by his superiors For some offense, not recorded but probably trivial enough, Fraser administered to Falardeau, one of his men, a French Canadian, so severe a castigation that death resulted It fell to one Baptiste, an Iroquois, to make the coffin for the murdered man, for no other term adequately covers the mode of Falardeau's death. While so engaged, planing and shaping the boards, Fraser passed by him and observing his occupation, roughly told him that "rough, unplaned boards are good enough for that rascal" Baptiste stared at Fraser a moment in amazement and then exclaimed with characteristic bluntness, "When you die you may not have even rough boards to be buried in." As though a spirit of prophesy had prompted the frank reply, two months later Fraser was suddenly killed while camped on Manson's Mountain, Similkameen, and buried on the spot without coffin of any description He was sitting in his tent reading, while his men were preparing their camp. Some of these were engaged in felling a large tree, which by some mischance crashed into the tent, crushing the life out of the man who had begrudged a few planed boards in the coffin of the man for whose death he was responsible.

There were three grades of officers in the Hudson's Bay Company's service clerk, chief trader and chief factor. Clerks received $100 to $150 a year with keep Promotion rarely came before 14 or 15 years service, the next step being to chief trader, who then became a shareholder instead of a salaried servant. After a further 15 to 20 years service came the coveted promotion to chief factor according to vacancies, these being infrequent. The chief trader had charge of a post, several such posts being under the direction of a chief factor.

CHAPTER VI.

DAWN OF A NEW ERA.

The Discovery of Gold —The Rush to the Fraser and
Cariboo—Trouble With the Indians—Commander
Mayne Visits Kamloops.

CHAPTER VI.

DAWN OF A NEW ERA.

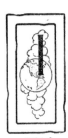 N the sixth decade of the 19th century a new era dawned upon the country. Hitherto the fur companies had monopolised it and their one object was to secure furs in as great abundance as possible. In the fifties however, the presence of gold in the streams and rivers became known and Chief Trader McLean, then in charge of Fort Kamloops, in 1852 purchased gold from the Indians who had obtained it from the Thompson river. It was at Nicomen, between Spence's Bridge and Lytton that gold in paying quantities was first discovered. Then from several quarters came the report of fresh discoveries. Halfbreeds and Canadians from Fort Colville, formerly in the employ of the Hudson's Bay Company, made their way to the vicinity of Lytton, found rich bars and their success becoming noised abroad soon brought new comers from afar. McDonald and Adams, two partners engaged in mining on the Thompson and Fraser in 1857-8 took some gold down to the lower country where McDonald killed Adams, took his gold

and coolly exhibited it at Olympia. The rush soon began
in earnest and in 1858 thousands of men over-ran the
Fraser river from its mouth to Lytton and above that
point on both the Fraser and Thompson rivers.

While thousands arrived from various ports, most of
them landing at Victoria and thence by what transportation was available to Fraser river points, a large number
made the journey overland from California. For protection against the Indians they found it advisable to
travel in companies, these being composed of from 400
to 500 men. The route taken was in the main, that
which Ross had followed forty years before when he
was almost the sole white man in the whole southern
interior of the country, by way of Okanagan and Kamloops. Some of them traveled with pack trains, others
with oxen, the latter sold for beef on arriving at the
mines. One of these companies from California and
Oregon was under the leadership of McLaughlin and
numbered 160 well armed men. At Walla Walla they
were informed of the hostile attitude of several power-
iul bands of Indians. Before reaching the Columbia one
of the party was killed by the natives and after crossing
the river, when about to traverse a defile McLaughlin
fortunately detected an Indian scout spying from behind
a rock Both sides of the pass were ambuscaded by the
Indians and severe fighting took place, three men being
killed and several severely wounded. While the engage-
ment was in progress a detachment crossed tthe river
to outflank the Indians and after setting fire to the grass
the latter abandoned their position. A few days later
the party suffered attack by mounted natives but ultimately a parley ensued and peace was patched up. It

Sir James Douglas.

was not of much force, for cattle were stolen and thefts
and annoyances of daily occurrence until within three
days journey of the Thompson river which they reached
at a point nearly midway between Lytton and Spence's
Bridge Others came by way of Okanagan lake and
Kamloops

The Victoria Gazette, the first newspaper published in
British Columbia of August 17, 1858, refers to one of
these overland parties as follows:—

"Our Yale correspondent states that Mr Tucker, formerly of Lehama, California, who had arrived at the Forks
(By this name the junction of the Thompson with the
Fraser at Lytton was then designated) in a company
of 160 men, with 400 animals, from the Dalles, had been
30 days on the trip, and had a severe fight with the Indians on the road at Fort Okanagan, an old Hudson's Bay
Company post, in which they lost three killed and six
wounded. Had beaten the Indians off with the loss of
five horses."

The fortune hunters who came overland made in the
main for two points, the Forks (Lytton) and the Fountain, above Lillooet. Those who came by sea and from
Washington Territory, mined in the vicinity of Hope
and Yale Twenty thousand men mined on the Fraser
and Thompson in 1858, the major portion of them between Hope and the Forks. As Hope was the point of
departure for the upper reaches by the Similkameen-Nic-
ola trail, besides being the then head of navigation, it
became the most important place on the mainland.
Townsites were laid out and surveyed at Langley, Hope
and Yale and lots were sold by auction, bringing good
prices A writer thus describes Yale as it was when he

DATE IN		DATE OUT		TOTAL NO. OF DAYS			PARK FEE	TOTAL RES.	TOTAL CASH PAID
MO.	DAY	MO.	DAY		C O D E				
13	05	14	05	1	5		11.50	11.50	

GST INCLUDED 438124

CHECK OUT TIME IS 11:00 a.m.
MUST VACATE SITE BY THIS TIME

USER OF THIS PERMIT ASSUMES ALL RISK OF
PERSONAL INJURY OR PERSONAL PROPERTY

Keep this portion for your records

PLEASE REMOVE THE PERMIT FROM THE NUMBER
POST WHEN YOU VACATE YOUR CAMPSITE

PLEASE RESPECT POSTED QUIET TIMES

OPERATOR'S G.S.T. NUMBER

saw it on July 28th, 1858. "We arrived at Fort Yale in a
little less than nine hours from Fort Hope. There are
probably 700 or 800 people here, nearly all of whom are
miners, living in canvas tents, and waiting for the river
to fall I saw no drunkeness or lawlessness of any kind.
Everything was peaceful and quiet A number of miners
were at work on the river bank, with rockers, and most
of them making a living by washing the loose dirt and
cobble stones." (At that time there were 2000 miners
working between Yale and Hope, taking out from $10
to $00 a day on the bars) "I slept at Mr. Johnson's (of
Ballou's express) tent that night and breakfasted next
morning with my old San Francisco friend, Henry M
Snyder, whom I found tenting a little way down the
river He gave me a good breakfast consisting of fried
salmon, bacon, hot bread and coffee, cooked by himself,
and served in tin plates and cups—each man sitting down
tailor fashion on the ground I had a sharp appetite
and did the fare full justice."

"There is but one public eating house in the town, and
the invariable diet is bacon, salmon, bread, tea and coffee,
and the charge is $1 a meal. No milk or butter is ever
seen. The eating house is kept in a log house partly covered with bark, and with a dirt floor.   Everything is done
in the same room, which is not more than 12 x 14 and is
consequently exceedingly cramped for space and as hot
as an oven." It was on that same day that the Uma-
tilla, the pioneer steamer to reach Yale, made her first
trip to that town, taking five hours to make the trip from
Hope; the return trip was made in 51 minutes, her advent being the occasion for general rejoicing, the miners
firing off rifles and revolvers and yelling themselves

hoarse to celebrate the event Yale then became the head of navigation and this speedily brought about a new order of things. The Hope route became a secondary matter and a reversion to the old Anderson route, pack trains between Yale and Spuzzum being in operation in the following month. At Spuzzum, Frank Way had erected a bridge and a mile above he ran a ferry The first pack trains over this route reached the Forks (Lytton) on September 10th There was, however, a rival road, a land and water route, between Harrison river and Lillooet. (In 1860 a new and better road was opened between Yale and Lytton, which afterwards became the famous Cariboo wagon road). The river was worked for 140 miles up-stream from Hope, and also up the Thompson to 15 miles beyond the confluence with the Nicola river. Boston Bar became quite a settlement, and by October, 1858, Lytton had 50 dwellings. Miners worked up above that town and by November there were 3,000 working near Fountain.

Commander Mayne describes Lytton, which he visited in 1859, as then consisting "of an irregular row of some dozen wooden huts, a drinking saloon, an express office, a large court-house—as yet unfinished—and two little buildings near the river, which had once belonged to the Hudson Bay Company, but which were now inhabited by the district magistrate The gentleman happened to be absent from Lytton, but I found his constable, and at once took up my quarters in the court house Next day, thinking we should find it preferable, we pitched our tent without, but the clouds of dust which swept over Lytton continuously soon made us glad to seek its shelter again"

But this had not all happened without some trouble

with the natives The Indians had taken to mining and
there were frequent disturbances between the natives
and the whites over mining ground and charges for
transportation by canoes. At Hill's Bar the natives
threatened to clear the entire country of the white men.
Governor Douglas rated both Indians and natives
roundly, but many a prospector who went up the Fraser
full of hope was never again seen On August 7th,,
1858, two Frenchmen were killed on the trail above the
Big Canyon. As soon as the news reached Yale forty
miners, well armed, and headed by Captain Rouse, left
for the scene of the murder. At Boston Bar they were
joined by 150 miners congregated there, and on the 14th
the party encountered the Indians at the head of the
canyon, a pitched battle took place and seven braves
were sent to the happy hunting grounds, and the Indians were driven out The party thereupon returned to
Yale. Referring to this expedition the Victoria Gazette
of 12th Sept., 1858, says:—

"Our Yale correspondent states that he learned from
James Stewart, who has just arrived from up river, that
after being perfectly satisfied that it was useless to
attempt to mine under the present state of affairs, his
party sold some of their provisions and buried the rest,
and started down the river for this place, when just at
the head of the Big Canyon they had a fight with the
Indians, killing nine, and among that number was one
chief Quite a number were wounded, and three taken
prisoners. The miners routed the Indians, who took
refuge in the mountains. Five of their rancheries were
burned."

Further fighting took place a few days later, but the

leader of the whites, H. M. Snyder, made treaties of
peace with all the Indians as far as the Thompson, and
soon the trail was alive with miners again. Early in
September, of the same year, Douglas again visited
Yale and for better preservation of the peace he appointed a commissioner, ten troopers and ten special
constables, a similar disposition was made at Hope, and
at Lytton a commissioner (Captain Trevallis), ten troopers and a warden of the river were appointed. Langley
was expected to be the capital of British Columbia, and
great preparations were made for the Royal Engineers
who were to be stationed there. In November, 1858,
they arrived, 25 of them, under Colonel Moody and
Captain Grant

The following January a report reached Victoria of
an outbreak at Yale Col Moody at once took his
whole force there and was reinforced by a party of
blue jackets and marines from the Satellite The difficulty, which arose out of a petty squabble, in which a
man named McGowan figured prominenttly, between a
couple of justices of the peace. Fortunately it ended
without any serious consequences, though it promised
at one time to be the cause of grave disturbance. It
was soon after this that the site of New Westminster
was examined by Lieutenant, afterwards Admiral,
Mayne and Dr Campbell on behalf of Col Moody.

After 1858 the Thompson, the first ground where gold
was mined, received but little attention and the mining
population was never great, though the gold was, and
is extensively distributed all along its course. In 1858,
Tranquille creek was prospected for a distance of 40
miles. In 1859 five men were making $300 a day with

sluice boxes, and others took out $10 to $12 a day with the rocker. In 1860 there were 200 Chinese mining at the mouth of the creek, and in the following year 150 miners averaged $16 a day in the vicinity of the creek. Up to this time, however, there was no mining done on the North river and save for the little done at Tranquille, Kamloops was out of the hurly burly that agitated the forts at Hope, Langley and Yale. The more peaceful and less exciting pursuit of trading with the Indians engaged the whole attention of the Hudson's Bay officers and men, and peace and quiet prevailed.

The condition of affairs at Kamloops in the year 1859, is well described by Commander Mayne of Her Majesty's ship Plumper, engaged in surveying, who made a trip through the districts bordering on the Fraser, Thompson and Harrison rivers. He says "It was eight o'clock in the morning when we came in sight of Kamloops The view from where we stood was very beautiful A hundred feet below us the Thompson, some 300 yards wide, flowed leisurely past us. Opposite, moving directly towards us, and meeting the larger river nearly at right angles, was the North river, at its junction with the Thompson, wider even than that stream, and between them stretched a wide delta of alluvial plain, which was continued some eight or ten miles until the mountains closed in upon the river so nearly, as to only just leave a narrow pathway by the water's edge At this fork, and on the west side stood Fort Kamloops, enclosed within pickets, and opposite it was the village of the Shuswap Indians. Both the plain and mountains were covered with grass and early spring wild flowers

We descended to the river side, and our Indian companions shouted until a canoe was sent across, in which we embarked and paddled across to the fort. Kamloops differed in no respect from other forts of the Hudson Bay Company that I had seen, being a mere stockade enclosing six or eight buildings, with a gateway at each end Introducing ourselves to Mr. McLean, the Company's officer in charge of the fort and district, we were most cordially received, and with the hospitality common to these gentlemen, invited to stay in his quarters for the few days we must remain here. At this time the only other officer at this fort was Mr Mason With them, however, was staying a Roman Catholic priest, who, having got into some trouble with the Indians of the Okanagan country, had thought it prudent to leave that district and take up his abode for a time at Kamloops.

"The life which these gentlemen lead at their inland stations must be necessarily dull and uneventful; but they have their wives and families with them, and grow, I believe, so attached to this mode of existence as rarely to care to exchange it for another. It may be well to describe here, in as few words as possible, the position of the Hudson Bay Company in these districts, of which until lately. they formed the sole white population. Those who have seen the "fur traders" only at their seaports, can form but a very inadequate idea of the men of the inland stations.

"Inland, you find men, who, having gone from England, or more frequently Scotland, as boys of 14 and 16, have lived ever since in the wild- never seeing any of their white fellow creatures but the two or three stationed with them, except when the annual fur brigade called at their posts They are almost all married and have large families, their wives being generally halfbreed children of the older servants of the Company Marriage has always been encouraged amongst them to the utmost, as it effectually attaches a man to the country, and tends to prevent any glaring immorality among the subordinates, which if not checked, would soon lead to an unsafe familiarity with the neighbouring Indians, and render the maintenance of the post very difficult, if not impossible.

"The day after our arrival at Kamloops, we went across North River to the Indian village, to pay a visit to the chief of the Shuswap tribe, who was described o us as being somewhat of a notability. Here was the site of the old fort of the North West Company which some twelve years back, after the murder of Mr Black (the officer in charge of it) by the Indians, had been removed by his successor to the opposite side of the river No doubt the old site was preferable to the new, which is subject to summer floods. Only the year before our visit indeed, all the floors had been started by the water, and the occupants of the fort buildings had to move about in canoes.

"The building into which we were introduced was more like a regular wooden house than an Indian hut, In the centre room, lying at length upon a mattress stretched upon the floor, was the chief of the Shuswap Indians. His face was a fine one, although sickness and pain had worn it away terribly His eyes were black, piercing and restless, his cheekbones high, and the lips, naturally thin and close, had that white, compressed look which tells

Lytton in 1859.

so surely of constant suffering. Such was St Paul, as the Hudson Bay Company called him, or Jean Baptiste Lolo, as he had been named by the Roman Catholic priests who were in this district many years before" This was the same Lolo with whom Mr. Tod had much experience Crippled as he was, the old chief accompanied Commander Mayne and Dr Campbell to the mountain already mentioned as overlooking the fort, which they ascended and which, in honor of their guide, they christened Mount St Paul. Near it stands another elevation named Roches des Femmes, from the fact that in summer the native women often frequented it to gather edible moss and wild berries. This moss or lichen, (L jubatus)' was prepared by being boiled and pressed into cakes, in which form it was eaten

"The interior of the hut is divided into compartments and, upon entering, you may see a fire burning in each, with six or eight individuals huddled about it—their dusky forms scarcely distinguishable in the clouds of white'blinding smoke' which had no other outlet than the door' or sometimes a hole in the roof. Their temporary hut is constructed of thin poles covered with mats, but these are generally used only in the summer, and upon their fishing expeditions and travels. It is not usual, however, from some superstitious reason, or because of sickness breaking out, to leave their village with everything standing, and never return to them."

Commander Mayne also mentions that he went "to see the bands of horses driven in, and those past work selected for food There were some two hundred or three hundred horses of all sorts and ages at the station. Just outside the fort were two pens, or corrals as they

called them, and into these the horses were driven. A
few colts were chosen for breaking in, and then the old
mares, whose breeding time was past, were selected
and—for it was upon horse flesh principally that the
people of the fort lived—driven out to be killed, skin-
ned and salted down."

Commander Mayne had a spice of the romantic in
his composition. He missed seeing the Fur Brigade—
which was daily expected at the time of his visit to Kamloops— and he says "It was not without regret that I
missed seeing the Fur Brigade It is one of those insti-
tutions of this wild and beautiful country, which must
give way before the approach of civilization. The time
will come—soon, perhaps—when such a sight as a train
of some 200 horses, laden with fur packages, winding
their way through the rough mountain passes of British
Columbia, will be as unfamiliar as that of a canoe upon
its rivers. No doubt the change will be for the better,
but it is sometimes hard to believe it Of course it is
much more practical to ascend the Fraser in a river steamboat than to make the journey in an Indian canoe * * *
but it will be long before I should prefer the former
method of locomotion to the latter when the weather is
fine With all its many inconveniences, there is something
marvellously pleasant in canoe travelling, with its tran-
quil, gliding motion, the regular, splashless dip, dip of
the paddles, the wild chant of the Indian crew, or better
still, the songs of the Canadian voyageurs, keeping time to
the pleasant chorus of "Ma Belle Rosa," or "Le Beau
Soldat."

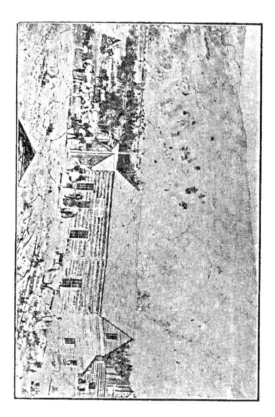

A Cariboo Road Hostelry—Cache Creek, 1863.

CHAPTER VII.

THE SEARCH FOR GOLD.

Excitement in Southern British Columbia—The Building
of the Cariboo Road—The First Passing of Yale.

CHAPTER VII.

THE SEARCH FOR GOLD.

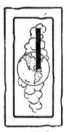

N 1861 the presence of gold in the bars of the North Thompson and its branches first attracted attention. Jameson Creek, Clearwater river, Barriere river (where a party of Frenchmen made $50 a day), Adams river, Moberly creek and other streams made things a little livelier around the old fort and in 1862 there was still a further addition by the arrival of an adventurous party who had made the long trip across the prairies and while a portion of the original party descended the Fraser to Quesnel, another portion followed the North River. Two of them were drowned and the remainder nearly perished for lack of food. Among them was one woman having in her care three children and adding to the number a few miles above Kamloops. Among those who came in this party were the late Samuel Moore, J. A. Mara, C. T. Cooney, G. C. Tunstall, the late James McIntosh, etc., each of whom has since that long ago day done his share to build up the town and vicinity.

Prior to the Fraser river excitement, gold was mined on the upper Columbia, as early indeed as 1856, Governor Douglas having in that year announced the fact to the Colonial Office. Miners earned from $10 to $40 a day, but with their usual restlessness and fickleness, the news of a new "strike" was sufficient to cause them to rush away to the new field. In 1863-4 an excitement was aroused over the placer ground in the Kootenay valley near the boundary line, but this was not so intens, as the Big Bend excitement which occurred shortly afterwards

Wild Horse Creek, a tributary of the Kootenay river, was the scene of the Kootenay flurry Discovered in 1863, in May 1864, four hundred miners had staked claims on it and, according to Hudson Bay Factor MacKay, by August, 5,000 men were in the district. One tenth of these remained for the winter at Fisherville the principal camp or town on the Creek which was reached by two routes, one from Colville via Pend d'Oreille,, the other from Fort Hope, via the Similkameen, Rock Creek and Pend d'Oreille In 1866, Fisherville was pulled down to allow the site to be mined Farms were located on the benches in the Kootenay Valley, and as the Indians there had an abundance of horses, the miners had no difficulty in moving from creek to creek to try for new ground, Perry Creek, where $18 to $30 a day to the man was taken out, being the chief.

Rock Creek, in 1860, was a busy mining centre, the creek near its mouth yielding from one to two ounces a day Mission Creek and several others emptying into

Yale in 1860.

Okanagan lake were all mined about the same date, 1859-61, from two dollars to forty dollars a day being obtained.

In 1863, the late Jos. W McKay was in charge of the Hudson's Bay fort at Kamloops and William G Cox held the office of gold commissioner and police magistrate at a salary of £400 a year. Yale Lytton and Lillooet each had its gold commissioner. In 1861, Kamloops was honored with a visit from Governor Douglas who made the trip by way of Kamloops, and Okanagan Lake to Rock Creek, returning by way of the Dewdney-Moberly trail, then nearly completed. In 1862 Douglas determined to build the wagon road along the Fraser There was already in use the water and land route via Harrison river to Douglas and Lillooet, in the construction of which 500 men—anxious to get to the Cariboo country where gold had then just been found—were employed, Governor Douglas agreeing to land at Douglas all provisions and supplies at Victoria prices if the men would turn to and build the road, all of which was done In 1862 the great rush to Cariboo was at its height and the projected new road along the Fraser was at once pushed A writer describing the road and Yale, its starting point, in 1863, says:—

"Since the Fraser River excitement of 1858, Yale has always been a hustling, busy little place, and notwithstanding the competition of the Douglas route, that via Yale has always retained its popularity." (This must have reference to the trails along the Fraser) "The great government works which have been carried on in the valley of the Fraser above Yale during the past summer, have had a beneficial effect on the prosperity of the place, and caused a considerable rise in the value of lots in the town By the middle of next May a road, passable for wagons, will have been completed from Yale to Williams creek (lake is no doubt meant) a distance of 160 miles. The road from Yale to Lytton (6; miles) which goes through the precipitous channel of the Fraser, known as the Big Canyon, has been con-structed at a great cost to the colony From Yale to Pike's Riffle, six miles and six chains, the road was built by the Royal Engineers; from Pike's Riffle to Chapman's bar, a distance of 8 miles, by Mr. (afterwards Sir J W) Trutch, for $47,000, from Chapman's Bar to Boston Bar, 11 to 12 miles, by Messers Spence and Trutch (the Spence here mentioned constructed the bridge over the Thompson river at the place which still is known as Spence's Bridge, though the bridge has long since been washed away) for $75,000, from Boston Bar to Lytton, 32 1-2 miles, by Mr Spence for $88,000, Mr. Spence employed 600 men on this work which he completed in four months The engineering difficulties encountered in carrying out the above work have been considerable, and a bridge has yet to be thrown across the river (Fraser) before the chain of communication is completed There is no doubt that this will become one of the main roads into the Interior of the country." Mr. Spence, in connection with Mr. Trutch, built the suspension bridge at Spuzzum across the Fraser and the new road was soon thronged with pack trains and heavily laden freight wagons bound for the Cariboo mines or the Hudson's Bay posts at Kamloops and elsewhere. The road is now a thing of the past; for since the C P R. came into being it is no longer passable;

Loading Freight at Yale, for Cariboo.

bridges have given way, rock slides block up the road-
way, cribbing has tumbled into the turbulent waters of
the Fraser, and the "old timer" who sees these things
mourns for the good old road and the good old days
spent on it.

With the working out of bar diggings in the vicinity
of Yale and the inauguration of regular stage lines to
Cariboo, Yale gradually lost a considerable part of her
population and the town lost much of its bustle and stir.
The forwarding of merchandise to Cariboo and other
intermediate points by pack trains, mule teams, ox teams
("bull teams" they were called) and other means of con-
veyance, engaged the attention of many men who have
since risen to prominence in the province and many way
side houses were kept for the public convenience, and
the proprietor's profit, by others who have attained a
like eminence.

In 1863 the Hudson's Bay Company again moved
their post at Kamloops, this time to the south bank,
opposite the second site, there they remained until the
march of progress rendered it advisable to make another
change and the building in the west end of the town recently occupied by the Standard, was erected in 1885.
In 1894 they moved to their present commodious quarters   In 1864 the Columbia river bars attracted attention
of the gold miners and with the discovery of gold in
the Big Bend a busy time came for Kamloops, which
was on the direct route of travel to the new mines. The
government opened a trail from Kamloops by way of
Shuswap Lake, and in 1866, the wagon road was extended
form Cache Creek to Savona at the foot of Kamloops
Lake. Meanwhile the H. B. Co., the late J. W. McKay

being then in charge, the only available local source of supplies, in anticipation of the rush, built the Steamer Marten during the winter of 1865. The following spring the rush began and the Marten made regular trips from Savona to Seymour, at the head of Shuswap Lake, the fare being $10 for passengers, and freight rates $20 a ton. Each trip the litle boat was crowded with miners, thousands flocked to the new mines and Seymour, form which point the rest of the journey was made by trail, became quite a thriving town, of which, however, little trace is left at this time. Kamloops gained some benefit from the excitement and the improvement was such that Messrs Mara and Wilson opened up a store in 1867. The Marten was the first steamer to ply on these waters and ascended the North River to a point 120 miles from its mouth. In 1868 Wm. Fortune, who built the first house in Kamloops, built the first flour mill in the interior of B. C., the burrs coming from Buffalo and costing $1,200 for the pair. A short time after the road was completed to Savona it was decided to extend it to Kamloops, and the late James McIntosh had the contract for building it.

CHAPTER VIII.

THE COMING OF THE RAILWAY.

End of the Crown Colony Days—British Columbia Be-
comes a Province—Growth of Kamloops.

Eagle Pass Landing as it was in 1885.

CHAPTER VIII.

THE COMING OF THE RAILWAY.

OWARDS the latter part of that memorable decade, the sixties, the question of confederation became a burning issue in the province and in 1868 we find that an important convention was held at Yale to consider the question, the gathering being attended by delegates from all parts of the province, those from the interior being from Yale, C. Evans, J. McLardy and H. Havelock; from Lytton, R. Smith; from Lillooet, Dr. Featherstone; from Lac la Hache, Dr. Brouse; from Williams Lake, Hon. F. Barnard; from Quesnelle Mouth, J. C. Armstrong; and from Cariboo, C. W. King and E. H. Rabbit. Resolutions were unanimously passed favoring immediate admission to the Dominion of Canada. This was the first representative assembly in B. C. at which this momentous issue was discussed. It was not, however, until 1871 that confederation was accomplished.

One of the conditions of the compact entered into by B. C. and the Dominion was the construction of a transcontinental railway. Of the disappointments and postponements and heartburnings before that condition was fulfilled there is no need to enlarge in this necessarily brief synopsis of events, suffice it to say that it was not until 1880 that the first sod of the C. P. P. was turned in the province but once begun, it was pushed vigorously. Andrew Onderdonk, familiarly referred to by everybody on or off the road as "A. O.," was the contractor and the amount involved for that portion of the road from Emory to Savona, including the cantilever bridge at Cisco, was $11,200,000, an average of $43,000 per mile. Over 7.000 men were employed, sawmills were built by the contractor, a powder factory was erected and operated between Yale and Emory, machine shops were built at Yale and although for a time the main offices were at Emory, it was soon found that Yale was better adapted for the management's headquarters and Yale once more put on the airs of a city, and the bustle and stir surpassed that of 20 years before It was a wide open town, money flowed like water, good wages were earned and freely spent and for a lively place, few western towns could compare with little resurrected Yale. Town property jumped to a high figure, business men put up stores and built residences, the regular steamboat connection with New Westminister was soon supplemented with trains—not very elegant affairs, with most uncomfortable coaches—from down the river, and as the road progressed eastward, by trains running in that direction as well.

Supplies for the road were taken partly by wagon, partly by pack train, but this was expensive and slow and finally it was decided to build a steamer to run the canyon of the Fraser and convey the supplies more economically to the farther camps. The steamer Skuzzy was built at the Big Tunnel, east of Spuzzum, and after

East Limit of Kanloops in 1884.

some difficulty a skipper was found willing to essay the task of taking the vessel through the boiling, eddying, treacherous rapids as they foamed through the dangerous canyon. Finally two brothers named Smith consented to try and with J. W. Burse as engineer, aided by a powerful steam winch and capstan and 150 Chinamen hauling on the ropes the first load of freight was safely carried and distributed along the river. Several trips were made up and down, Lytton being the farthest point reached. Subsequently the Skuzzy was tied up at Keefer's and there remained until 1884, when the machinery was removed, taken to Savona and placed in the newly built hull of the Skuzzy number two.

With the passing of the period of activity coincident with railway construction, Yale again fell into desuetude, quiet reigned where bustle had prevailed; the streets, once thronged with men, became deserted, and gradually sinking farther and farther from the halycon days of yore, houses, deserted and desolate, sank into decay; stores, offices and warehouses, cheerless and empty, gave silent witness of a greatness that had been but was not. Twice Yale rose to a state of prosperity and affluence and twice has it fallen into peaceful rest; who will say it may not again become and permanently remain a hive of industry? Yale but experienced the same fate that befell many other towns. Lytton, too, was once a bustling little town, so were Savona, Ashcroft and Spence's Bridge. Eagle Pass Landing at the head of Shuswap lake shared the same fate that came to them all save Ashcroft, varied only in degree. But such places as endured have flourished, striking examples of the survival of the fittest.

In 1868 John Peterson pre-empted a parcel of land east of the then little village, and afterwards purchased an additional 320 acres. On the pre-emption he built a house and stables, which are still standing, a short distance east of the railway station. This location is of interest as this land, the Peterson ranch, constitutes the new town of Kamloops. In 1870 Barnard's express stages, carrying the mails, ran as far as Savona, the system soon extended to Kamloops and finally to Okanagan mission. The difficulty in procuring lumber led to the establishment of a new industry about 1875, when a combined flour and lumber mill was built on the flat, then east of the town. Messrs Mara, Wilson, McIntosh and Usherwere the owners. The last named gentleman was the government agent at Kamloops at that time, and met an untimely death, while engaged in the performance of his duty, at the hands of the McLean and Hare gang, four in number, in December, 1879. The murderers were hanged at New Westminster, January 31, 1881

The year 1878 saw another steamer built on these waters, the Lady Dufferin, the property of Wm. Fortune. The boat d d a general carrying business, running between Savona and Spallumcheen. The Spallumcheen, owned by Mara & Wilson, also plied on the same waters for a number of years.

Apart from the settlement that had been quietly and steadily going on in the district for some time, another important factor was at work in this decade in assisting to build up Kamloops, and this was the fact that from its position Kamloops would be a place of some importance on the line of the proposed Canadian Pacific Rail-

Kamloops in 1884.

way. It had been the intention to carry the road out to the coast at Bute Inlet, and in 1872 surveyors were sent out to survey the North Thompson and to explore for a route from the Clearwater to the Cariboo wagon road, with the view of getting to Bute Inlet via Chilcotin, but this idea was abandoned and it was ultimately decided to bring the line down the North Thompson to Kamloops and then carry it to the salt water by the route since adopted. Lord Dufferin visited Kamloops in 1876.

Kamloops was given telegraphic communication in 1878, the line being built by the Liberal Government under Premier Alex. Mackenzie F. J. Barnard, who afterwards sat in the House of Commons as representative for Yale district, was the contractor for this work.

Kamloops was now fairly on her feet, and boasted of hotels as well as stores. The Dominion Hotel was in the hands of McIntosh & Mc Phadden, and 'he Cosmopolitan was conducted by John Peterson & Dawsonville. Mara & Wilson had the only store in the village, the Hudson's Bay Company's store being some little distance west of it, where near the bridge the old buildings are yet standing. In 1880 there were three stores, three hotels, two blacksmith shops and a school. Father Grandidier was the first resident clergyman taking up his abode in Kamloops in 1878. He and other visiting clergymen attended to the spiritual welfare of the people. In that year, A. Watson, of Victoria, built the Peerless steamboat for J. A. Mara to run, according to the Colonist, "between Cook's Ferry and the head of navigation" The Peerless made a trip to Harper's mill, at the mouth of the Bonaparte (near Ashcroft), in June,

1881, without using a line on the journey, accomplishing
the distance, 20 miles up stream, in five hours, and
subsequently made one trip to Cook's Ferry (Spence's
Bridge), Captain John Irving being in command. Kamloops reached out for trade in those days, perhaps pro-
portionately more than today, although trade was not
always of the briskest. The Standard (a Victoria newspaper that long ago ceased to have its being), in the
issue of June 12, 1880, says: "Times at Kamloops are
dull at present. The Shuswap mill has been under
water for the past month. The Tranquille mill is running night and day. The steamer Lady Dufferin is
making regular trips every Tuesday to Spallumcheen.
Large quantities of flour are being shipped from Tranquille mill to Savona's Ferry, Cariboo and other places."

In December, 1880, J F McCreight was appointed a
judge for the inland country, to sit at Kamloops.

May, 1881, saw Major Rogers set out from Kamloops
by steamer to Eagle river to look for a pass through
the Selkirk range for the C. P. R. construction on
which was now going forward with vigor. A pass was
subsequently found, and the route was again changed
The Yellow Head Pass was abandoned, and an entirely
new route was selected, the line reaching Kamloops by
the South Thompson instead of by the North branch. At
about the same time in the press the claims of Kamloops
as the proper capital of the Mainland were put forward
and discussed.

In the same year increased mail service was given
to points east, reached by wagon road from Kamloops.
So far a semi-monthly mail had been given, but in the
spring of 1881 the mail contract from Cache Creek

to Okanagan Mission (now known as Kelowna), via Kamloops and Spallumcheen, giving a weekly service for four years, was awarded to J. B. Leighton

The Province was in 1882 in the throes of the fourth general election (Provincial) since Confederation, and Mr. Mara was elected for the third consecutive term, with him being associated Preston Bennett, who had represented the same district in the previous legislature, and C. A. Semlin, who was one of the trio selected from Yale to represent that district in the first legislature of the conjoint Province. Mr. Bennett never sat in the fourth parliament, for a few days after the election he had an attack of hemorrhage of the lungs, and died on August 9, 1882, at the residence of Mr. John Tait, local manager of the Hudson's Bay Company's post since 1872. The vacancy caused by Mr. Bennett's death was filled by G. B. Martin, who continued to represent Yale until the general election of 1898, when he was defeated by F. J. Deane, who in turn was defeated in 1900 and 1903 by F. J. Fulton.

CHAPTER IX.

FROM FORT TO CITY.

Social Life in Old Kamloops—Setting Out the New
Town—Incorporation.

CHAPTER IX.

FROM FORT TO CITY.

OCIAL life in the earlier days was not marked by the lines that characterize it to-day.
The people were almost like one family, and
at times they met for jollity and pleasure;
balls and impromptu dances in winter,
horse-racing and other sports on such public
holidays as were observed. But a change
was at hand. The C. P. R. was coming
slowly but steadily nearer. The shrill
whistle of the locomotive was soon heard
at Savona, and in the winter of 1884
the grading of the roadbed between that point and
Kamloops was under way. Kamloops was now a busy
place, with a constant stream of people going and coming, and it was not without its distinguished visitors.
October, 1882, had seen the Marquis of Lorne in Kamloops and three years later the Marquis of Lansdowne,
his successor to the Governor-Generalship, visited the
town.

Up to 1884 no newspaper had been published at
Kamloops, but in that year the Inland Sentinel made
its appearance as a Kamloops publication. This was

not, however, the beginning of the paper. Mr. Hagan, its founder, first established the paper at Emory, a few miles below Yale, on May 29, *1880, removing to Yale shortly afterwards. Moving with the times and the railway, Mr. Hagan brought the Inland Sentinel to Kamloops, where it has remained.

In that same year the first firemen's company was established, the meetings at which it was formed being held in Spelman's (Cosmopolitan) hotel, in August. The following month a movement was set on foot to build a hospital in Kamloops. Arrangements were soon made, and the contract for the building was given to W. A. Simmons. The hotels in 1884 were of some importance, for half the population lived in them. The Arlington, near where the Queen's hotel now stands, was kept by Sears & Nichols. At a later date the building was removed bodily to the east end of the street and was named the Oriental, now Leland hotel, Frank Rushton doing the honors as host for a time. Jos. Ratchford, recently the superintendent of the Provincial home, ran the Kamloops house. The late Ed. Cannell had the Dominion, J. T. Edwards the Cosmopolitan and Desormier the Colonial The medical profession was represented by Dr. S. J. Tunstall, now of Vancouver, and Dr. Offerhaus, now of Spallumcheen. It was a treat to see the latter, clad in his dressing gown, stalk down to the stables through the only street Kamloops then possessed, to feed and groom his little cayuse. W. W. Spinks, now judge of the county court, was then practising as an attorney, and for some time was the only member of the bar in town. The housekeeper of the present day would be staggered were our storekeepers to revert to the prices of 1884. Flour was $6 per 100 lbs.; ham and bacon 30 cents per lb.; tea 80 cents to $1.50 per lb.; pork 25 cents; sugar 25 cents and eggs 75 cents a dozen. Hay sold at $25 per ton, and lumber at $20 to $30 per thousand.

A visitor in Oct., 1884, was Hon. Wm. Smythe, then Premier, who was also Chief Commissioner of Lands and Works, which latter portfolio, after his death in 1887, fell to F. G. Vernon, one of the three members for Yale district, which then for the first time secured cabinet representation.

The next year saw many advances made. The Hudson's Bay people moved their store into the town. A new steamer, the Kamloops, was built early in the year, and was launched in April, the machinery being that from the Myra, a stern-wheeler that had formerly run below Yale.

Failing to come to an arrangement with Mr. Mara for the transport of supplies, Mr. Onderdonk determined to build a steamer to ply on these waters, using the machinery from a discarded steamer, the Skuzzy, which had made several eventful trips through the canyon of the Fraser. A hull was built at Savona, the machinery installed, and then a compromise arranged. The Skuzzy was put to good use, however, serving as a floating hotel for the tracklayers, and moving along with them, as they came on towards and beyond Kamloops. The Skuzzy was afterwards bought by Mr. Mara, and is now lying beside the Peerless, sheer hulks.

In July, 1885, the railway track reached Kamloops, and on November 7th of the same year, at 3 o'clock in the afternoon, the first through train from the east to Port Moody arrived

In the same year John Peterson disposed of his ranch lying to the east of the old town to the townsite syndicate, of which Messrs. Mara, Ward and Pooley were members. The new townsite was surveyed at once by R. H. Lee. In 1885 the Government decided to build a new court house Government Agent Tunstall chose the present central site, and in that same year its construction was entered upon. The old court house destroyed by fire three years ago, was a log cabin, white washed, with the cells opening direct into the confined space that served as court room, in which, indeed, many matters of grave moment have come before the judges of both the County and Supreme courts Court day was deemed a sort of festival, and the coming of a Supreme court judge—and Mr Justice Walkem was the favorite—was looked forward to with a zest that is not seen in the present and more prosaic age.

With the coming of the C. P. R., the town grew steadily, and its being made a divisional point at once added largley to its growing population In early days, water was carried from the river in buckets, or hauled up in barrels, but with the growth of the town these means became altogether inadequate. The late Mr.McIntosh, who was never lacking in enterprise, met the want and supplied the town from a reservoir into which the water was pumped from the river. By private enterprise also the town was supplied with electric light. In 1893 the city was incorporated, and the water and light services were acquired by the municipality by purchase. Two new plants have since been put in.

In 1896 the presence of copper-gold ore was discovered on Coal hill, not far from the place where a few years previously Major Vaughan and others had mined with more or less success for coal Development has progressed steadily and the Iron Mask mine is now a regular shipper, and other properties give indications of arriving at the same stage in the near future.

But little mention has been made of local representation in the House of Commons Dominion elections created very little excitement until the last two or three contests Chas F. Houghton was first chosen, but his term was short, the parliament only lasting 1871-72. He was succeeded by Edgar Dewdney (afterwards Lieut-governor of the province), who sat for Yale from 1872 until his appointment as Indian commissioner. F. J Barnard stepped into his shoes, to be himself replaced by J A. Mara, who occupied the seat from 1886 until his defeat by Mr. Bostock at the general election, 1896, in the united constituency of Yale-Cariboo. In the general election of 1900, W. A Galliher of Nelson, was elected M. P., and in 1904, the district being divided into two constituencies, Kootenay and Yale-Cariboo, Duncan Ross was elected for the latter, H. Bostock being created a senator in the same year.

APPENDIX TO CHAPTER TWO.

Alexander Ross. then in the service of the Pacific Fur Company, first visited the vicinity of where Kamloops now stands on May 16th, 1812. He had been preceded, however, by David Thompson, the Nor'wester, who explored the Thompson river early in 1811, and David Stuart, one of the partners in the Pacific Fur Company. On September 16th, 1811, Stuart, accompanied by three men, two of whom, Montigny and Boullard, were Canadian voyageurs, left Fort Okanagan, near the junction of the Okanagan and Columbia rivers, on a journey to the unexplored north, leaving Alexander Ross, mentioned above, alone in charge of the then newly established post, his sole "civilized companion being,' as Ross puts it, "a little Spanish pet dog from Monterey, named Weasel."

Intending only to be absent a month, it was not until March 22nd, 1812, that Stuart and his companions returned to Fort Okanagan. Of his journey he gave the following account. "After leaving this place" (Fort Okanagan) "we bent our course up the Oakinacken, due north, for upwards of 250 miles, till we reached its source: then crossing a height of land fell upon Thompson's River, or rather the south branch of Fraser's River, after travelling for some time amongst a powerful nation called the She Waps (Shuswaps) The snow fell while we were here in the mountains, and precluded our immediate return; and after waiting for fine weather the snow got so deep that we considered it hopeless to attempt to get back, and, therefore, passed our time with the She Waps and other tribes in that quarter. The Indians were numerous and well disposed, and the country throughout abounds in beavers and all other kinds of fur: and I have made arrangements to establish a trading post there the ensuing winter. On the 2nth of February we began our homeward journey, and spent just twenty-five days on our way back. The distance may be about 350 miles."

Early in 1812, the first meeting of the partners in the Pacific Fur Company was held at Fort Astoria, and among the resolutions passed was this one. "That Mr David Stuart proceed to his post at Oakinacken, explore the country northward, and establish another post between that and New Caledonia." The new post suggested in this resolution was to be at Kamloops and thither Mr Stuart despatched Alexander Ross. Ross thus describes the expedition —

"On the 6th of May I started with Boullard and an Indian, with sixteen horses, on a trading excursion, and following Mr. Stuart's route of last winter, reached the She Waps on Thompson's River, the tenth day, and there encamped at a place called by the Indians Cumcloups, near the entrance of the North branch. From this station I sent messages to the different tribes around, who soon assembled, bringing with them their furs. Here we stayed for ten days. The number of Indians collected on the occasion could not have been less than 2,000," (and the one white man, Ross, alone amongst them with his trading outfit!) "Not expecting to see so many, I had taken but a small quantity of goods with me; nevertheless, we loaded all our horses—so anxious were they to trade, and so fond of leaf tobacco, that one morning before breakfast I obtained one hundred and ten beavers for leaf tobacco, at the rate of five leaves per skin, and at last, when I had but one yard of white cotton remaining, one of the chiefs gave me twenty prime beaver skins for it. Having finished our trade, we prepared to return home; but before we could get our odds and ends ready, Boullard, my trusty second, got involved in a love affair, which had nearly involved us all in a disagreeable scrape with the Indians. He was as full of latent tricks as a serpent is full of guile. Unknown to me, the old fellow had been teasing the Indians for a wife, and had already an old squaw at his heels, but could not raise the wind to

pay the whole purchase money With an air of effrontery
he asked me to unload one of my horses to satisfy the de-
mands of the old father-in-law, and because I refused him,
he threatened to leave me and to remain with the savages.
Provoked by his conduct, I suddenly turned round and
horsewhipped the fellow, and, fortunately, the Indians did
not interfere The castigation had a good effect, it brought
the amorous gallant to his senses—the squaw was left
behind. ''

In the same year, on August 25th, Mr. Stuart, with men
and merchandise, set out from Oakinacken for "She Waps,"
and four months later, December 20th, Mr. Ross, who had
been again left in charge of Fort Oakinacken, left the fort
to pay a visit to his chief at "Cumeloups," where he arrived
on the last day of 1812. He found that Mr. Stuart had just
established himself in his winter quarters, and that the
Northwest Company following hard on his heels, had built
a post alongside of him, "so that," wrote Ross, "there
was opposition there as well as at Mr. Clarke's place, without the trickery and manoeuvring M. La Roque, the
Northwest clerk in charge, and Mr. Stuart were open and
candid and on friendly terms." With Mr Stuart, Ross re
mained for five days, and then returned to Fort Oakinacken,
following a new route. He wrote: "But I chose a bad season
of the year to satisfy my curiosity We got bewildered in
the mountains and deep snows, and our progress was exceedingly slow, tedious and discouraging. We were five
days in making as many miles." After suffering hunger
and privations, shared by man and beast, Ross reached an
Indian camp where a day was spent to recuperate, "procured some furs, and then, following the course of the Sim-
ilka-meigh river, got to Oakinacken at the forks," reaching
the fort on January 24th, 1813

On May 13th Mr. Stuart with his men and furs, arrived at
Fort Okanagan from the "She Waps," in reference to which
post he wrote: "I have passed a winter nowise unpleasant.
the opposition, it is true, gave me a good deal of anxiety
when it first arrived, but we agreed very well, and made as

much, perhaps more, than if we had been enemies   I sent
out parties in all directions, north as far as Fraser's River,
and for 200 miles up the south branch   The accounts from
all quarters were most satisfactory.   The country is every-
where rich in furs and the natives very peaceable "

CPSIA information can be obtained
at www.ICGtesting.com
Printed in the USA
LVHW080622220221
679513LV00006B/769

9 780342 768448